Discovering po

Monique Horsfall
July 1979.

Discovering poetry

selected by E W Parker
revised by Michael Marland

Book 1
Book 2
Book 3
Book 4 (Fresh fields)

Companion series

Enjoying poetry

selected by E W Parker

1 Silver and gold
2 For delight
3 For your pleasure
4 A galaxy of poems old and new

Discovering poetry 3

chosen by E W Parker
the collection revised by Michael Marland

Longman

LONGMAN GROUP LIMITED
London

Associated companies, branches and representatives throughout the world

First published 1953
Tenth impression 1967
Second edition 1971
Second impression 1974
Third impression 1977

ISBN 0 582 21904 3

Printed in the Republic of Singapore by Chong Moh Offset Printing Pte. Ltd.

The poems

Youth remembered

Tyne Dock Francis Scarfe 1
A recollection Frances Cornford 2
The rock pool Philip Hobsbaum 2
A tropical childhood Edward Lucie-Smith 3
My parents kept me from children who were rough Stephen Spender 4
Mid-term break Seamus Heaney 4
The lesson Edward Lucie-Smith 5
The collier Vernon Watkins 6

The family circle

The sick wife Unknown Chinese poet 8
The collier's wife D H Lawrence 9
My grandmother Elizabeth Jennings 11
Night song David Holbrook 12
Hide and seek Vernon Scannell 13
Discord in childhood D H Lawrence 14
Unholy marriage David Holbrook 14
Under the mountain Louis MacNeice 16
On a friend's escape from drowning off the Norfolk coast George Barker 17

The natural world

Weather ear Norman Nicholson 18
Considering the snail Thom Gunn 18
The summer shower John Clare 19
The woodman and his dog William Cowper 23
The vagabond Robert Louis Stevenson 24
The gallows Edward Thomas 25
Wind Ted Hughes 26
Storm in the Black Forest D H Lawrence 27
At day-close in November Thomas Hardy 28

The city world

Preludes	T S Eliot	29
The days of the week in eighteenth-century London	John Gay	30
A description of a city shower	Jonathan Swift	31
London	A S J Tessimond	32
Leaving town	James Reeves	32

Press and placard

Advertising	A S J Tessimond	34
The great newspaper editor to his subordinate	D H Lawrence	34
Editorial impressions	Siegfried Sassoon	36

Ships and the sea

The seafarer	Unknown Anglo Saxon author, trans. Ezra Pound	37
Sir Patrick Spens	Not known	38
Oh that men would praise the Lord!	The Bible	41
The rime of the ancient Mariner	Samuel Taylor Coleridge	42
Storm off the Suffolk coast	George Crabbe	63
Relic	Ted Hughes	64

Into battle

Blow, bugle, blow	Lord Tennyson	65
My brother was a pilot	Bertolt Brecht	65
Five minutes after the air raid	Miroslav Holub	66
War chant	African song	67
Lament of the frontier guard	Rihaku	68
The companion	Yevgeny Yevtushenko	69
The battle of Stamford Bridge	Laurence Binyon	70
An incident of the French camp	Robert Browning	74
At fifteen I went with the army	Unknown Chinese poet	75
Death of an aircraft	Charles Causley	76
O Captain! My Captain!	Walt Whitman	78
Children's crusade 1939	Bertolt Brecht	79

Domestic laughter

The old cloak	Not known	86
The diverting history of John Gilpin	William Cowper	88
Sir Smasham Uppe	E V Rieu	97
Domestic asides	Thomas Hood	98
The wee cooper o' Fife	Not known	99

Three legends

Queen Mab	Ben Jonson	101
The Faerie Queene	Edmund Spenser	102
The ballad of Richard Peake	Lord Rennell of Rodd	103

Life and death

Prayer before birth	Louis MacNeice	111
Four orders	Ronald Bottrall	112
Pilgrim's song	John Bunyan	113
For his mercy endureth for ever	The Bible	114
The King of glory shall come in	The Bible	115
Magnificat	Book of Common Prayer	116
A living	D H Lawrence	117
My busconductor	Roger McGough	117
Days	Philip Larkin	118
The song of the mad prince	Walter de la Mare	119
Death	Traditional African poem	120

The poets

Barker, George (born 1913) 17
Binyon, Laurence (1869–1943) 70
Bottrall, Ronald (born 1906) 112
Brecht, Bertolt (1898–1956) 65, 79
Browning, Robert (1812–1889) 74
Bunyan, John (1628–1688) 113
Causley, Charles (born 1917) 76
Clare, John (1793–1864) 19
Coleridge, Samuel Taylor (1772–1834) 42
Cornford, Frances (1886–1960) 2
Cowper, William (1731–1800) 23, 88
Crabbe, George (1754–1832) 63
de la Mare, Walter (1873–1956) 119
Eliot, T S (1888–1964) 29
Gay, John (1685–1732) 30
Gunn, Thom (born 1929) 18
Hardy, Thomas (1840–1928) 28
Heaney, Seamus (born 1939) 4
Hobsbaum, Philip (born) 2
Holbrook, David (born 1923) 12, 14
Holub, Miroslav (born 1923) 66
Hood, Thomas (1799–1845) 98
Hughes, Ted (born 1930) 26, 64
Jennings, Elizabeth (born 1926) 11
Jonson, Ben (1573–1637) 101
Larkin, Philip (born 1922) 118
Lawrence, D H (1885–1930) 9, 14, 27, 34, 117
Lucie-Smith, Edward (born 1933) 3, 5
MacNeice, Louis (1907–1974) 16, 111
McGough, Roger (born 1938) 117
Nicholson, Norman (born 1914) 18
Reeves, James (born 1909) 32
Rennell, Lord Rennell of Rodd (1858–1941) 103

Rieu, E V (born 1887) 97
Rihaku (eighteenth century) 68
Sassoon, Siegfried (1886-1967) 36
Scannell, Vernon (born 1922) 13
Scarfe, Francis (born 1911) 1
Spender, Stephen (born 1901) 4
Spenser, Edmund (1552-1599) 102
Stevenson, Robert (1850-1894) 24
Swift, Jonathan (1667-1745) 31
Tennyson, Lord (1809-1892) 65
Tessimond, A S J (born 1902) 32, 34
Thomas Edward (1878-1917) 25
Watkins, Vernon (1906-1967) 6
Whitman, Walt (1819-1892) 78
Yevtushenko, Yevgeny (born 1933) 69

Acknowledgements

We are grateful to the following for permission to use copyright material: Barrie & Jenkins Ltd. for 'A Recollection' by Frances Cornford; Cambridge University Press for 'War Chant' from *African Poetry* by Beier; author, author's agents and Rupert Hart Davis for 'Death of an Aircraft' by Charles Causley from *Union Street*; Constable & Co. Ltd. for 'At Fifteen I went with the Army' and 'The Sick Wife' from *170 Chinese Poems* translated by Arthur Waley; Eyre & Spottiswoode for extracts from Psalms from the Authorised Version of the Bible, which is Crown Copyright in England; Faber & Faber Ltd. and Harper & Row of New York for 'Wind' from *The Hawk in the Rain* by Ted Hughes, Harper & Row, Copyright 1956 by Ted Hughes; Faber & Faber Ltd. and New Directions Publishing Corporation, New York for 'Lament of the Frontier Guard' translated by Ezra Pound from *Collected Shorter Poems*, Ezra Pound Personae, Copyright 1926 by Ezra Pound; Faber & Faber Ltd. for 'Considering the Snail' from *My Sad Captains* by Thom Gunn, 'Relic' by Ted Hughes from *Lupercal*, 'Days' by Philip Larkin from *The Whitsun Weddings*, 'Mid-term Break' by Seamus Heaney from *Death of Naturalist*, 'Weather Ear' by Norman Nicholson from *The Pot Geranium*, 'Preludes' by T S Eliot from *Collected Poems 1909–1962*, 'The Seafarer' by Ezra Pound from *The Translations of Ezra Pound*, Prayer before Birth' and 'Under the Mountain' by Louis MacNeice from *Collected Poems*, 'My Parents kept me from children who were rough' by Stephen Spender from *Collected Poems 1928–1953*, 'The Collier' by Vernon Watkins from *Ballad of the Mari Lwyd*, 'On a friend's escape from drowning off the Norfolk coast' by George Barker; William Heinemann Ltd for 'Leaving Town' from *Collected Poems by James Reeves*; Author for 'Unholy Marriage' by David Holbrook from *Imaginings*; Hope Leresche & Steele, for 'My Busconductor' by Roger McGough; author, author's agents and Macmillan & Co. Ltd. for 'My Grandmother' from *Collected Poems*; The Estate of the late Mrs Frieda Lawrence, and author's agents for 'The Collier's Wife', 'Discord in Childhood', Storm in the Black Forest', 'The Great Newspaper Editor to his Subordinate' and 'A Living' by D H Lawrence from *Complete Poems*; Macmillan & Co. Ltd. for 'The Rock Pool' by Philip Hobsbaum from *In Retreat*; The Trustees of the Hardy Estate, The Macmillan Company of Canada Ltd. and Macmillan & Co. Ltd. for 'At Day-close in November' by Thomas Hardy; Methuen & Co. Ltd. for 'Children's Crusade 1939' and 'My

Brother was a Pilot' by Bertolt Brecht and 'Sir Smasham Uppe' by E V Rieu from *The Flattered Flying Fish*; Hubert Nicholson for 'Advertising' and 'London' both from *Voices in a Giant City* by A S J Tessimond; Oxford University Press for 'The Summer Shower' by John Clare from *Selected Poems and Prose of John Clare* edited by Eric Robinson and Geoffrey Summerfield; and 'A Tropical Childhood' and 'The Lesson' by Edward Lucie-Smith from *A Tropical Childhood and Other Poems*; Penguin Books Ltd. for 'The Companion' by Yevgeny Yevtushenko translated by Robin Milner-Gulland and Peter Levi, S J and 'Five Minutes after the Air Raid' by Miroslav Holub translated by Ian Milner and George Theiner; Putnam & Co. for 'Night Song' by David Holbrook from *Against the Cruel Frost*; the author for 'Hide and Seek' from *Walking Wounded* by Vernon Scannell; the author for 'Tyne Dock' by Francis Scarfe; the executors of the estate of Siegfried Sassoon for 'Editorial Impressions' by Siegfried Sassoon from *Collected Poems 1908–1956*; Sidgwick & Jackson Ltd. for 'Four Orders' by Ronald Bottrall from *Collected Poems 1961*; Mrs Nicolete Gray and The Society of Authors, on behalf of the Laurence Binyon Estate for 'The Battle of Stamford Bridge' by Laurence Binyon; The Literary Trustees of Walter de la Mare and the Society of Authors as their representative for 'The Song of the Mad Prince' by Walter de la Mare.
We have been unable to trace the copyright holder of 'Death' by an unknown African poet which was first published in a Jeune Afrique and would appreciate any information which would enable us to do so.

The cover picture is Sanby's *The Ancient Beech Tree* and is reproduced by kind permission of the Trustees of the Victoria and Albert Museum.

Tyne Dock

The summer season at Tyne Dock
Lifted my boyhood in a crane
Above the shaggy mining town,
Above the slaghills and the rocks,
Above the middens in backlanes
And wooden hen-huts falling down.

Grass grew vermilion in the streets
Where the blind pit-ponies pranced
And poppies screamed by butchers' stalls
Where bulls kicked sparks with dying feet,
And in the naked larks I sensed
A cruel god beneath it all.

Over the pithead wheel the moon
Was clean as a girl's face in school;
I envied the remote old man
Who lived there, quiet and alone,
While in the kitchen the mad spool
Unwound, as Annie's treadle ran.

The boyish season is still there
For clapping hands and leaping feet
Across the slagheaps and the dunes,
And still it breaks into my care
Though I will never find the street,
Nor find the old, impulsive tune,
Nor ever lose that child's despair.

Francis Scarfe

A Recollection

My father's friend came once to tea.
He laughed and talked. He spoke to me.
But in another week they said
That friendly pink-faced man was dead.

'How sad . . .' they said, 'the best of men. . . .'
So I said too, 'How sad', but then
Deep in my heart I thought, with pride,
'I know a person who has died'.

Frances Cornford

The rock pool

My life could have ended then, crouched over the pool,
Wedged against Huntcliff. Absorbed in its own life,
Its pimpled sea-fronds and the slimy rocks
Spangled with barnacles, the pool lay
Deceptively clear to the sky, its wraiths of weed,
its floating upturned dead snails, the limpets
Solidly bossed[1] to the rock – I tried to prise them
Into a free float, but cut my fingers
And winced. Deep in the clefts still with mussels
I pried, and under the weed that carpeted
The pool bottom recoiled from a starfish, waylaid
A crab – there he glared, squeezed little face
Tucked under his shell. And never noticed till
A wave sploshed into my pool, stirring up sludge,

[1] stuck on like a knob

Swathing crab, starfish, limpets too, in fog,
That the tide had come up, to my ears soundlessly,
Warning me off to my world, away from the sea.

Philip Hobsbaum

A tropical childhood

In the hot noons I heard the fusillade
  As soldiers on the range learnt how to kill,
Used my toy microscope, whose lens arrayed
  The twenty rainbows in a parrot's quill.

Or once, while I was swimming in the bay,
  The guns upon the other, seaward shore
Began a practice-shoot; the angry spray
  Fountained above the point at every roar.

Then I, in the calm water, dived to chase
  Pennies my father threw me, searched the sand
For the brown disc a yard beneath my face,
  And never tried to see beyond my hand.

That was the time when a dead grasshopper
  Devoured by ants before my captive eye
Made the sun dark, yet distant battles were
  Names in a dream, outside geography.

Edward Lucie-Smith

My parents kept me from children who were rough

My parents kept me from children who were rough
Who threw words like stones and who wore torn clothes.
Their thighs showed through rags. They ran in the street
And climbed cliffs and stripped by country streams.

I feared more than tigers their muscles like iron
Their jerking hands and their knees tight on my arms.
I feared the salt coarse pointing of those boys
Who copied my lisp behind me on the road.

They were lithe, they sprang out behind hedges
Like dogs to bark at my world. They threw mud
While I looked the other way, pretending to smile.
I longed to forgive them, but they never smiled.

Stephen Spender

Mid-term break

I sat all morning in the college sick bay
Counting bells knelling classes to a close.
At two o'clock our neighbours drove me home.

In the porch I met my father crying –
He had always taken funerals in his stride –
And Big Jim Evans saying it was a hard blow.

The baby cooed and laughed and rocked the pram
When I came in, and I was embarrassed
By old men standing up to shake my hand

And tell me they were 'sorry for my trouble',
Whispers informed strangers I was the eldest,
Away at school, as my mother held my hand

In hers and coughed out angry tearless sighs.
At ten o'clock the ambulance arrived
With the corpse, stanched and bandaged by the nurses.

Next morning I went up into the room. Snowdrops
And candles soothed the bedside; I saw him
For the first time in six weeks. Paler now,

Wearing a poppy bruise on his left temple,
He lay in the four foot box as in his cot.
No gaudy scars, the bumper knocked him clear.

A four foot box, a foot for every year.

Seamus Heaney

The lesson

'Your father's gone,' my bald headmaster said.
His shiny dome and brown tobacco jar
Splintered at once in tears. It wasn't grief.
I cried for knowledge which was bitterer
Than any grief. For there and then I knew
That grief has uses – that a father dead
Could bind the bully's fist a week or two;
And then I cried for shame, then for relief.

I was a month past ten when I learnt this:
I still remember how the noise was stilled
In school-assembly when my grief came in.
Some goldfish in a bowl quietly sculled
Around their shining prison on its shelf.
They were indifferent. All the other eyes
Were turned towards me. Somewhere in myself
Pride, like a goldfish, flashed a sudden fin.

Edward Lucie-Smith

The collier

When I was born on Amman hill
A dark bird crossed the sun.
Sharp on the floor the shadow fell;
I was the youngest son.

And when I went to the County School
I worked in a shaft of light.
In the wood of the desk I cut my name:
Dai for Dynamite.

The tall black hills my brothers stood;
Their lessons all were done.
From the door of the school when I ran out
They frowned to watch me run.

The slow grey bells they rung a chime
Surly with grief or age.
Clever or clumsy, lad or lout,
All would look for a wage.

I learnt the valley flowers' names
And the rough bark knew my knees.
I brought home trout from the river
And spotted eggs from the trees.

A coloured coat I was given to wear
Where the lights of the rough land shone.
Still jealous of my favour
The tall black hills looked on.

They dipped my coat in the blood of a kid
And they cast me down a pit,
And although I crossed with strangers
There was no way up from it.

Soon as I went from the County School
I worked in a shaft. Said Jim,
'You will get your chain of gold, my lad,
But not for a likely time.'

And one said, 'Jack was not raised up
When the wind blew out the light
Though he interpreted their dreams
And guessed their fears by night.'

And Tom, he shivered his leper's lamp
For the stain that round him grew;
And I heard mouths pray in the after-damp
When the picks would not break through.

They changed words there in darkness
And still through my head they run,
And white on my limbs is the linen sheet
And gold on my neck the sun.

Vernon Watkins

The sick wife

She had been ill for years and years;
She sent for me to say something.
She couldn't say what she wanted
Because of the tears that kept coming of themselves.
'I have burdened you with orphan children,
With orphan children two or three.
Don't let our children go hungry or cold;
If they do wrong, don't slap or beat them.
When you take out the baby, rock it in your arms.
Don't forget to do that.'
Last she said,
'When I carried them in my arms they had no clothes
And now their jackets have no linings.' [*She dies.*

I shut the door and barred the windows
And left the motherless children.
When I got to the market and met my friends, I wept.
I sat down and could not go with them.
I asked them to buy some cakes for my children.
In the presence of my friends I sobbed and cried.
I tried not to grieve, but sorrow would not cease.
I felt in my pocket and gave my friends some money.
When I got home I found my children
Calling to be taken into their mother's arms.
I walked up and down in the empty room
This way and that a long while.
Then went away from it and said to myself
'I will forget and never speak of her again.'

Unknown Chinese author
translated by Arthur Waley

The collier's wife

Somebody's knockin' at th' door
    Mother, come down an' see!
– I's think it's nobbut a beggar;
    Say I'm busy.

It's not a beggar, mother; hark
    How 'ard 'e knocks!
– Eh, tha'rt a mard-arsed kid,
    'E'll gie thee socks!

Shout an' ax what 'e wants,
    I canna come down.
– 'E says, is it Arthur Holliday's?
    – Say Yes, tha clown.

'E says: Tell your mother as 'er mester's
    Got hurt i' th' pit –
What? Oh my Sirs, 'e never says that.
    That's not it!

Come out o' th' way an' let me see!
    Eh, there's no peace!
An' stop thy scraightin', childt,
    Do shut thy face!

'Your mester's 'ad a accident
    An' they ta'ein' 'im i' th' ambulance
Ter Nottingham.' – Eh dear o' me,
    If 'e's not a man for mischance!

Wheer's 'e hurt this time, lad?
    – I dunna know,
They on'y towd me it wor bad –
    It would be so!

Out o' my way, childt! dear o' me, wheer
'Ave I put 'is clean stockin's an' shirt?
Goodness knows if they'll be able
To take off 'is pit-dirt!

An' what a moan 'e'll make! there niver
Was such a man for fuss
If anything ailed 'im; at any rate
I shan't 'ave 'im to nuss.

I do 'ope as it's not very bad!
Eh, what a shame it seems
As some should ha'e hardly a smite o' trouble
An' others 'as reams!

It's a shame as 'e should be knocked about
Like this, I'm sure it is!
'E's 'ad twenty accidents, if 'e's 'ad one;
Owt bad, an' it's his!

There's one thing, we s'll 'ave a peaceful 'ouse f'r a bit,
Thank heaven for a peaceful house!
An' there's compensation, sin' it's accident,
An' club-money – I won't growse.

An' a fork an' a spoon 'e'll want – an' what else?
I s'll never catch that train!
What a traipse it is, if a man gets hurt!
I sh'd think 'e'll get right again.

D H Lawrence

My Grandmother

She kept an antique shop – or it kept her.
Among Apostle spoons and Bristol glass,
The faded silks, the heavy furniture,
She watched her own reflection in the brass
Salvers and silver bowls, as if to prove
Polish was all, there was no need of love.

And I remember how I once refused
To go out with her, since I was afraid.
It was perhaps a wish not to be used
Like antique objects. Though she never said
That she was hurt, I still could feel the guilt
Of that refusal, guessing how she felt.

Later, too frail to keep a shop, she put
All her best things in one long narrow room.
The place smelt old, of things too long kept shut,
The smell of absences where shadows come
That can't be polished. There was nothing then
To give her own reflection back again.

And when she died I felt no grief at all,
Only the guilt of what I once refused.
I walked into her room among the tall
Sideboards and cupboards – things she never used
But needed: and no finger-marks were there,
Only the new dust falling through the air.

Elizabeth Jennings

Night song

Stack the cups and clear away;
The bonfire sinks to ash;
Daytime is so much trash,
Night climbs the stairway.

We have done what we can to use the light,
Cricket and jar take over;
Children snore, the smell of clover
Tickles the poacher's nose as he treads it over.

Poppy and rose swim in the warm remainder,
Exhausted current of day;
Cold comes down from the air, hay
Hears warm in the field what the lovers say.

Bare to the teeming black the heady tree
Sighs in its sleep and stirs;
Softly an owl-wing whirrs,
The water chuckles, the paper beetle burrs.

Stack the cups and clear away,
The bonfire sinks to ash;
Daylight is so much trash,
Night climbs the stairway.

David Holbrook

Hide and seek

Call out. Call loud: 'I'm ready! Come and find me!'
The sacks in the toolshed smell like the seaside.
They'll never find you in this salty dark,
But be careful that your feet aren't sticking out.
Wiser not to risk another shout.
The floor is cold. They'll probably be searching
The bushes near the swing. Whatever happens
You mustn't sneeze when they come prowling in.
And here they are, whispering at the door;
You've never heard them sound so hushed before.
Don't breathe. Don't move. Stay dumb. Hide in your blindness.
They're moving closer, someone stumbles, mutters,
Their words and laughter scuttle, and they're gone.
But don't come out just yet; they'll try the lane
And then the greenhouse and back here again.
They must be thinking that you're very clever,
Getting more puzzled as they search all over.
It seems a long time since they went away.
Your legs are stiff, the cold bites through your coat,
The dark damp smell of sand moves in your throat.
It's time to let them know that you're the winner.
Push off the sacks. Uncurl and stretch. That's better.
Out of the shed and call to them: 'I've won!
Here I am! Come and own up I've caught you!'
The darkening garden watches. Nothing stirs.
The bushes hold their breath, the sun is gone.
Yes, here you are. But where are they who sought you?

Vernon Scannell

Discord in childhood

Outside the house an ash-tree hung its terrible whips,
And at night when the wind rose, the lash of the tree
Shrieked and slashed the wind, as a ship's
Weird rigging in a storm shrieks hideously.

Within the house two voices arose, a slender lash
Whistling she-delirious rage, and the dreadful sound
Of a male thong booming and bruising, until it had drowned
The other voice in a silence of blood, 'neath the noise of the ash.

D H Lawrence

Unholy marriage

Police are seeking to identify the pillion rider who was also killed

Her mother bore her, father cared
And clothed her body, young and neat.
The careful virgin had not shared
Cool soft anointment of her breast
Or any other sweet,
But kept herself for best.

How sweet she would have been in bed,
Her bridegroom sighing in her hair,
His tenderness heaped on her head,
Receiving benediction from her breast
With every other fair
She kept for him, the best.

Who she is now they do not know
Assembling her body on a sheet.
This foolish virgin shared a blow
That drove her almost through a stranger's breast
And all her sweet
Mingles with his in dust.

Unwilling marriage, her blood runs with one
Who bought for a few pounds and pence
A steel machine able to 'do a ton',
Not knowing at a ton a straw will pierce a breast:
No wheel has built-in sense,
Not yet the shiniest and best.

And so, 'doing a ton', in fog and night
Before he could think, Christ! or she could moan
There came a heavy tail without a light
And many tons compressed each back to breast
And blood and brain and bone
Mixed, lay undressed.

Anointed only by the punctured oil
Poured like unleashed wind or fire from bag
Sold by some damned magician out to spoil
The life that girded in this young girl's breast,
Now never to unfurl her flag
And march love's happy quest.

Her mother hears the clock; her father sighs,
Takes off his boots: she's late tonight.
I hope she's careful virgin: men have eyes
For cherished daughters growing in the breast.
Some news? They hear the gate.
A man comes: not the best.

David Holbrook

Under the mountain

Seen from above
The foam in the curving bay is a goose-quill
That feathers . . . unfeathers . . . itself.

Seen from above
The field is a flap and the haycocks buttons
To keep it flush with the earth.

Seen from above
The house is a silent gadget whose purpose
Was long since obsolete.

But when you get down
The breakers are cold scum and the wrack
Sizzles with stinking life.

When you get down
The field is a failed or a worth-while crop, the source
Of back-ache if not heart-ache.

And when you get down
The house is a maelstrom of loves and hates where you –
Having got down – belong.

Louis MacNeice

On a friend's escape from drowning off the Norfolk coast

Came up that cold sea at Cromer like a running grave
    Beside him as he struck
Wildly towards the shore, but the blackcapped wave
    Crossed him and swung him back,
And he saw his son digging in the castled dirt that could save.
    Then the farewell rock
Rose a last time to his eyes. As he cried out,
    A pawing gag of the sea
Smothered his cry and he sank in his own shout
    Like a dying airman. Then she
Deep near her son asleep on the hourglass sand
    Was awakened by whom
Save the Fate who knew that this was the wrong time:
    And opened her eyes
On the death of her son's begetter. Up she flies
    Into the hydra-headed
Grave as he closes his life upon her who for
    Life has so richly bedded him.
But she drove through his drowning like Orpheus and tore
    Back by the hair
Her escaping bridegroom. And on the sand their son
    Stood laughing where
He was almost an orphan. Then the three lay down
    On that cold sand,
Each holding the other by a living hand.

George Barker

Weather ear

Lying in bed in the dark, I hear the bray
Of the furnace hooter rasping the slates, and say:
'The wind will be in the east, and frost on the nose, today.'

Or when, in the still, small, conscience hours, I hear
The market clock-bell clacking close to my ear:
'A north-west wind from the fell, and the sky-light swilled and clear.'

But now when the roofs are sulky as the dead,
With a snuffle and sniff in the gullies, a drip on the lead:
'No wind at all, and the street stone-deaf with a cold in the head.'

Norman Nicholson

Considering the snail

The snail pushes through a green
night, for the grass is heavy
with water and meets over
the bright path he makes, where rain
has darkened the earth's dark. He
moves in a wood of desire,

pale antlers barely stirring
as he hunts. I cannot tell
what power is at work, drenched there
with purpose, knowing nothing.
What is a snail's fury? All
I think is that if later

I parted the blades above
the tunnel and saw the thin
trail of broken white across
litter, I would never have
imagined the slow passion
to that deliberate progress.

Thom Gunn

The summer shower[1]

I love it well oercanopied in leaves
Of crowding woods to spend a quiet hour
And where the woodbine weaves
To list the summer shower

Brought by the south west wind that balm and bland
Breaths luscious coolness loved and felt by all
While on the uplifted hand
The rain drops gently fall

Now quickening on and on the pattering woods
Receives the coming shower birds trim their wings
And in a joyful mood
The little wood chat sings

And blackbird squatting in her mortared nest
Safe hid in ivy and the pathless wood
Pruneth her sooty breast
And warms her downy brood

[1] This poem is printed here with the spelling and punctuation as it appears in the poet's manuscript

And little Pettichap[1] like hurrying mouse
Keeps nimbling near my arbour round and round
Aye there's her oven house[1]
Built nearly on the ground

Of woodbents withered straws and moss and leaves
And lined with downy feathers safteys joy
Dwells with the home she weaves
Nor fears the pilfering boy

The busy falling rain increases now
And sopping leaves their dripping moisture pour
And from each loaded bough
Fast falls the double shower

Weed climbing hedges banks and meeds unmown
Where rushy fringed brooklet easy curls
Look joyous while the rain
Strings their green suit [with] pearls

While from the crouching corn the weeding troop
Run hastily and huddling in a ring
Where the old willows stoop
Their ancient ballads sing

And gabble over wonders ceaseless tale
Till from the south west sky showers thicker come
Humming along the vale
And bids them hasten home

With laughing skip they stride the hasty brook
That mutters through the weeds untill it gains
A clear and quiet nook
To greet the dimpling rain

[1] The garden warbler (pettichap) builds a dome- or oven-shaped nest

And on they drabble[1] all in mirth not mute
Leaving their footmarks on the elting[2] soil
Where print of sprawling foot
Stirs up a tittering smile

On beautys lips who slipping mid the crowd
Blushes to have her anckle seen so high
Yet inly feeleth proud
That none a fault can spy

Yet rudely followed by the meddling clown
Who passes vulgar gibes – the bashful maid
Lets go her folded gown
And pauses half afraid

To climb the stile before him till the dame
To quarrel half provoked assails the knave
And laughs him into shame
And makes him well behave

Bird nesting boys oertaken in the rain
Beneath the ivied maple bustling run
And wait in anxious pain
Impatient for the sun

And sigh for home yet at the pasture gate
The molehill tossing bull with straining eye
Seemeth their steps to wait
Nor dare they pass him bye

Till wearied out high over hedge they scrawl[3]
To shun the road and through the wet grass roam
Till wet and draggled all
They fear to venture home

[1] wade or splash about in water or mud
[2] soft
[3] clear the throat noisily

The plough team wet and dripping plashes home
And on the horse the ploughboy lolls along
Yet from the wet grounds come
The loud and merry song

Now neath the leafy arch of dripping bough
That loaded trees form oer the narrow lane
The horse released from plough
Naps the moist grass again

Around their blanket camps the gipseys still
Heedless of showers while black thorns shelter round
Jump oer the pasture hills
In many an idle bound

From dark green clumps among the dripping grain
The lark with sudden impulse starts and sings
And mid the smoaking rain
Quivers her russet wings

A joy inspiring calmness all around
Breaths a refreshing sense of strengthening power
Like that which toil hath found
In sundays leisure hour

When spirits all relaxed heart sick of toil
Seeks out the pleasant woods and shadowy dells
And where the fountain boils
Lye listening distant bells

Amid the yellow furze the rabbits bed
Labour hath hid his tools and oer the heath
Hies to the milking shed
That stands the oak beneath

And there he wiles the pleasant shower away
Filling his mind with store of happy things
Rich crops of corn and hay
And all that plenty brings

The crampt horizon now leans on the ground
Quiet and cool and labours hard employ
Ceases while all around
Falls a refreshing joy

John Clare

The woodman and his dog

Forth goes the woodman, leaving unconcerned
The cheerful haunts of man, to wield the axe
And drive the wedge in yonder forest drear,
From morn to eve his solitary task.
Shaggy, and lean, and shrewd, with pointed ears
And tail cropped short, half lurcher and half cur,
His dog attends him. Close behind his heel
Now creeps he slow; and now with many a frisk
Wide scampering, snatches up the drifted snow
With ivory teeth, or ploughs it with his snout;
Then shakes his powdered coat, and barks for joy.
Heedless of all his pranks, the sturdy churl
Moves right toward the mark; nor stops for aught,
But now and then with pressure of his thumb
To adjust the fragrant charge of a short tube
That fumes beneath his nose: the trailing cloud
Streams far behind him, scenting all the air.

William Cowper

The vagabond

Give to me the life I love,
    Let the lave[1] go by me,
Give the jolly heaven above
    And the byway nigh me.
Bed in the bush with stars to see,
    Bread I dip in the river –
There's the life for a man like me,
    There's the life for ever.

Let the blow fall soon or late,
    Let what will be o'er me;
Give the face of earth around
    And the road before me.
Wealth I seek not, hope nor love,
    Nor a friend to know me;
All I seek, the heaven above,
    And the road below me.

Or let autumn fall on me
    Where afield I linger,
Silencing the bird on tree,
    Biting the blue finger,
White as meal the frosty field –
    Warm the fireside haven –
Not to autumn will I yield,
    Not to winter even!

Let the blow fall soon or late,
    Let what will be o'er me;
Give the face of earth around
    And the road before me.

[1] the rest (Scottish)

Wealth I ask not, hope nor love,
  Nor a friend to know me;
All I ask, the heaven above,
  And the road below me.

Robert Louis Stevenson

The gallows

There was a weasel lived in the sun
With all his family,
Till a keeper shot him with his gun
And hung him up on a tree,
Where he swings in the wind and rain,
In the sun and in the snow,
Without pleasure, without pain,
On the dead oak tree bough.

There was a crow who was no sleeper,
But a thief and a murderer
Till a very late hour; and this keeper
Made him one of the things that were,
To hang and flap in rain and wind,
In the sun and in the snow.
There are no more sins to be sinned
On the dead oak tree bough.

There was a magpie, too,
Had a long tongue and a long tail;
He could both talk and do –
But what did that avail?
He, too, flaps in the wind and rain
Alongside weasel and crow,
Without pleasure, without pain,
On the dead oak tree bough.

And many other beasts
And birds, skin, bone and feather,
Have been taken from their feasts
And hung up there together,
To swing and have endless leisure
In the sun and in the snow,
Without pain, without pleasure,
On the dead oak tree bough.

Edward Thomas

Wind

This house has been far out to sea all night,
The woods crashing through darkness, the booming hills,
Wind stampeding the fields under the windows
Floundering black astride and blinding wet

Till day rose. Then, under an orange sky,
The hills had new places, and wind wielded
Blade-light, luminous black and emerald
Flexing like the lens of a mad eye.

At noon I scaled along the house-side as far as
The coal-house door. I dared once to look up:
Through the brunt wind that dented the balls of my eyes
The tent of the hills drummed and strained its guy-rope,

The fields quivering, the skyline a grimace,
At any second to bang and vanish with a flap:
The wind flung a magpie away, and a black
Back gull bent like an iron bar slowly. The house

Rang like some fine green goblet in the note
That any second would shatter it. Now deep
In chairs, in front of the great fire, we grip
Our hearts and cannot entertain book, thought,

Or each other. We watch the fire blazing,
And feel the roots of the house move, but sit on,
Seeing the window tremble to come in,
Hearing the stones cry out under the horizons.

Ted Hughes

Storm in the Black Forest

Now it is almost night, from the bronzey soft sky
jugfull after jugfull of pure white liquid fire, bright white
tipples over and spills down,
and is gone
and gold-bronze flutters beat through the thick upper air.

And as the electric liquid pours out, sometimes
a still brighter white snake wriggles among it, spilled
and tumbling wriggling down the sky:
and then the heavens cackle with uncouth sounds.

And the rain won't come, the rain refuses to come!

This is the electricity that man is supposed to have mastered
chained, subjugated to his own use!

supposed to!

D H Lawrence

At day-close in November

The ten hours' light is abating,
And a late bird wings across,
Where the pines, like waltzers waiting,
Give their black heads a toss.

Beech leaves, that yellow the noon-time,
Float past like specks in the eye;
I set every tree in my June time,
And now they obscure the sky.

And the children who ramble through here
Conceive that there never has been
A time when no tall trees grew here,
That none will in time be seen.

Thomas Hardy

Preludes

I

The winter evening settles down
With smell of steaks in passageways.
Six o'clock.
The burnt-out ends of smoky days.
And now a gusty shower wraps
The grimy scraps
Of withered leaves about your feet
And newspapers from vacant lots;
The showers beat
On broken blinds and chimney-pots,
And at the corner of the street
A lonely cab-horse steams and stamps.
And then the lighting of the lamps.

II

The morning comes to consciousness
Of faint stale smells of beer
From the sawdust-trampled street
With all its muddy feet that press
To early coffee-stands.
With the other masquerades
That time resumes,
One thinks of all the hands
That are raising dingy shades
In a thousand furnished rooms.

T S Eliot

The days of the week in eighteenth-century London

Experienc'd men, inur'd[1] to city ways,
Need not the Calendar to count their days.
When through the town with slow and solemn air,
Led by the nostril, walks the muzled bear;
Behind him moves majestically dull,
The pride of Hockley-hole, the surly bull;
Learn hence the periods of the week to name,
Mondays and Thursdays are the days of game.
When fishy stalls with double store are laid;
The golden-belly'd carp, the broad-finn'd maid,
Red-speckled trouts, the salmon's silver joul,
The joynted lobster, and unscaly soale,
And luscious 'scallops, to allure the tastes
Of rigid zealots to delicious fasts;
Wednesdays and Fridays you'll observe from hence,
Days, when our sires were doom'd to abstinence.
When dirty waters from balconies drop,
And dext'rous damsels twirle the sprinkling mop,
And cleanse the spatter'd sash, and scrub the stairs;
Know Saturday's conclusive morn appears.

John Gay

[1] used, accustomed

from
A description of a city shower

Now in contiguous[1] Drops the Flood comes down,
Threat'ning with Deluge this Devoted Town.
To Shops in Crouds the daggled Females fly,
Pretend to cheapen Goods, but nothing buy.
The Templer[2] spruce, while ev'ry Spout's[3] a-broach,
Stays till 'tis fair, yet seems to call a Coach.
The tuck'd-up Semptstress[4] walks with hasty Strides,
While Streams run down her oil'd Umbrella's Sides.
Here various Kinds by various Fortunes led,
Commence Acquaintance underneath a Shed.

Now from all Parts the swelling Kennels[5] flow,
And bear their Trophies with them as they go:
Filth of all Hues and Odours seem to tell
What Street they sail'd from, by their Sight and Smell.
They, as each Torrent drives, with rapid Force
From Smithfield, or St Pulchre's shape their Course,
And in huge Confluent join at Snow-Hill Ridge,
Fall from the Conduit prone to Holborn-Bridge.
Sweepings from Butchers Stalls, Dung, Guts, and Blood,
Drown'd Puppies, stinking Sprats, all drench'd in Mud,
Dead Cats and Turnip-Tops come tumbling down the Flood.

Jonathan Swift

[1] joined together
[2] a law student from the part of London called the Temple
[3] the roof pipes which poured rainwater onto the streets
[4] sewing woman
[5] gutters

London

I am the city of two divided cities
Where the eyes of rich and poor collide and wonder;
Where the beggar's voice is low and unexpectant,
And in clubs the feet of the servants are soft on the carpet
And the world's wind scarcely stirs the leaves of *The Times*.

I am the reticent, the private city,
The city of lovers hiding wrapped in shadows,
The city of people sitting and talking quietly
Beyond shut doors and walls as thick as a century,
People who laugh too little and too loudly,
Whose tears fall inward, flowing back to the heart.

I am the city whose fog will fall like a finger gently
Erasing the anger of angles, the strident indecorous gesture,
Whose dusk will come like tact, like a change in the conversation,
Violet and indigo, with strings of lemon streetlamps
Casting their pools into the pools of rain
As the notes of the piano are cast from the top-floor window
Into the square that is always Sunday afternoon.

A S J Tessimond

Leaving town

It was impossible to leave the town.
Bumping across a maze of obsolete rails
Three times we reached the gasworks and reversed.
We could not get away from the canal;
Dead cats, dead hopes, in those grey deeps immersed,
Over our efforts breathed a spectral prayer.

The cattle-market and the gospel-hall
Returned like fictions of our own despair,
And like Hesperides[1] the suburbs seemed,
Shining far off towards the guiltless fields.
We finished in a little cul-de-sac
Where on the pavement sat a ragged girl
Mourning beside a jug-and-bottle entrance.
Once more we turned the car and started back.

James Reeves

[1] a mythical garden of golden apples, supposed to be at the extreme west of the earth

Advertising

You, without gleam or glint or fire,
You cannot know your own desire.
But I will tell you. I will look through your eyes. Now listen!
Here are the toys that please, the almost-gems that glisten! . . .
I am your wish and I its answer.
I am the drum and you the dancer.
I am the trumpet-voice, the Stentor.
I am temptation, I the Mentor
Who tells you that ten million men have long
Called a stone bread – and can ten million men be wrong?
I am the voice that bids you spend to save and save to spend,
But always spend that wheels may never end
Their turning and by turning let you spend to save
And save to spend, world without end, cradle to grave.

A S J Tessimond

The great newspaper editor to his subordinate

Mr Smith, Mr Smith
haven't I told you to take the pith
and marrow and substance out of all
the articles passing beneath your scrawl?

And now look here what you've gone and done!
You've told them that life isn't really much fun,
when you know that they've got to think that they're happy,

as happy as happy, Oh, so happy, you sappy.
Think of the effect on Miss Harrison
when she reads that her life isn't really much fun.
She'll take off her specs and she'll put down the paper
as if it was giving off poison vapour.

And she'll avoid it; she'll go and order
The Morning Smile, sure that it will afford her
comfort and cheer, sure that it will tell her
she's a marv'lous, delicious, high-spirited feller.

You must chop up each article, make it pappy
and easy to swallow; always tell them they're happy,
suggest that they're spicy, yet how *pure* they are,
and what a sense of true humour they've got, ha-ha!

Mr Smith, Mr Smith,
have you still to learn that pith
and marrow and substance are sure to be
indigestible to Miss Ponsonby!

Mr Smith, Mr Smith
if you stay in my office, you've got to be kith
and kin with Miss Jupson, whose guts are narrow
and can't pass such things as substance and marrow.

Mr Smith, Mr Smith
consider Miss Wilks, or depart forthwith.
For the British Public, once more be it said,
is summed up in a nice, narrow-gutted old maid.

D H Lawrence

Editorial impressions

He seemed so certain 'all was going well',
As he discussed the glorious time he'd had
While visiting the trenches.
'One can tell
You've gathered big impressions!' grinned the lad
Who'd been severely wounded in the back
In some wiped-out impossible Attack.
'Impressions? Yes, most vivid! I am writing
A little book called *Europe on the Rack*,
Based on notes made while witnessing the fighting.
I hope I've caught the feeling of "the Line",
And the amazing spirit of the troops.
By Jove, those flying-chaps of ours are fine!
I watched one daring beggar looping loops,
Soaring and diving like some bird of prey.
And through it all I felt that splendour shine
Which makes us win.'
The soldier sipped his wine.
'Ah, yes, but it's the Press that leads the way!'

Siegried Sassoon

The seafarer

May I for my own self song's truth reckon,
Journey's jargon, how I in harsh days
Hardship endured oft.
Bitter breast-cares have I abided,
Known on my keel many a care's hold,
And dire sea-surge, and there I oft spent
Narrow nightwatch nigh the ship's head
While she tossed close to cliffs. Coldly afflicted,
My feet were by frost benumbed.
Chill its chains are; chafing sighs
Hew my heart round and hunger begot
Mere-weary mood. Lest man know not
That he on dry land loveliest liveth,
List how I, care-wretched, on ice-cold sea,
Weathered the winter, wretched outcast
Deprived of my kinsmen;
Hung with hard ice-flakes, where hail-scur flew,
There I heard naught save the harsh sea
And ice-cold wave, at whiles the swan cries,
Did for my games the gannet's clamour,
Sea-fowls' loudness was for me laughter,
The mews' singing all my mead-drink.
Storms, on the stone-cliffs beaten, fell on the stern
In icy feathers; full oft the eagle screamed
With spray on his pinion.

Unknown Anglo-Saxon writer
translated by Ezra Pound

Sir Patrick Spens

The Sailing

The king sits in Dunfermline town
Drinking the bluid-red wine;
'O whare will I get a skeely[1] skipper
To sail this new ship o' mine?'

O up and spake an eldern knight,
Sat at the king's right knee;
'Sir Patrick Spens is the best sailor
That ever sailed the sea.'

Our king has written a braid letter,
And sealed it with his hand,
And sent it to Sir Patrick Spens,
Was walking on the strand.

'To Noroway, to Noroway,
To Noroway o'er the foam;
The king's daughter o' Noroway,
'Tis thou maun bring her home.'

The first word that Sir Patrick read
So loud, loud laughed he;
The neist word that Sir Patrick read
The tear blinded his e'e.

'O wha is this has done this deed
And told the king o' me,
To send us out, at this time o' year,
To sail upon the sea?

[1] skilful

'Be it wind, be it weet, be it hail, be it sleet,
Our ship must sail the foam;
The king's daughter o' Noroway,
'Tis we must fetch her home.'

They hoist their sails on Monday morn
Wi' a' the speed they may:
They hae landed in Noroway
Upon a Wodensday.

The Return

'Mak ready, mak ready, my merry men a'!
Our guide ship sails the morn.'
'Now ever alack, my master dear,
I fear a deadly storm.

'I saw the new moon late yestreen
Wi' the auld moon in her arm;
And if we gang to sea, master,
I fear we'll come to harm.'

They hadna sail'd a league, a league,
A league, but barely three,
When the lift[1] grew dark, and the wind blew loud
And gurly grew the sea.

The anchors brake, and the topmast lap,
It was sic a deadly storm:
The waves came owre the broken ship
Till a' her sides were torn.

'Go fetch a web o' the silken cloth,
Another o' the twine,
And wap[2] them into our ship's side,
And let na the sea come in.'

[1] the sky
[2] wrap

They fetch'd a web o' the silken cloth,
Another o' the twine,
And they wapp'd them round that gude ship's side,
But still the sea came in.

O loath, loath were our gude Scots lords
To wet their cork-heel'd shoon;
But land or a' the play was play'd
They wat their hats aboon.

And money was the feather bed
That flattered[1] on the foam;
And mony was the gude lord's son
That never mair came home.

O lang, lang may the ladies sit,
Wi' their fans into their hand,
Before they see Sir Patrick Spens
Come sailing to the strand!

And lang, lang may the maidens sit
Wi' their gowd combs in their hair
A-waiting for their ain dear loves!
For them they'll see nae mair.

Half owre, half owre to Aberdour
'Tis fifty fathom deep;
And there lies gude Sir Patrick Spens
Wi' the Scots lords at his feet!

Not known

[1] tossed afloat

Oh that men would praise the Lord!

They that go down to the sea in ships,
That do business in great waters;
These see the works of the Lord,
And His wonders in the deep.
For He commandeth, and raiseth the stormy wind,
Which lifteth up the waves thereof.
They mount up to the heaven, they go down again to the depths
Their soul is melted because of trouble.
They reel to and fro, and stagger like a drunken man,
And are at their wit's end.
Then they cry unto the Lord in their trouble,
And He bringeth them out of their distresses.
He maketh the storm a calm,
So that the waves thereof are still.
Then are they glad because they be quiet;
So He bringeth them unto their desired haven.

Oh that men would praise the Lord for His goodness,
And for His wonderful works to the children of men!

From Psalm 107, *Authorised Version of the Bible*

The rime of the ancient Mariner

PART ONE

It is an ancient Mariner,
And he stoppeth one of three.
'By thy long grey beard and glittering eye,
Now wherefore stopp'st thou me?

'The Bridegroom's doors are opened wide,
And I am next of kin;
The guests are met, the feast is set:
May'st hear the merry din.'

He holds him with his skinny hand;
There was a ship, *quoth he.*
'Hold off! unhand me, grey-beard loon!'
Eftsoons his hand dropt he.

He holds him with his glittering eye –
The Wedding-Guest stood still,
And listens like a three years' child:
The Mariner hath his will.

The Wedding-Guest sat on a stone;
He cannot choose but hear;
And thus spake on that ancient man,
The bright-eyed Mariner.

The ship was cheered, the harbour cleared,
Merrily did we drop
Below the kirk, below the hill,
Below the lighthouse top.

The sun came up upon the left,
Out of the sea came he!
And he shone bright, and on the right
Went down into the sea.

Higher and higher every day,
Till over the mast at noon –
The Wedding-Guest here beat his breast,
For he heard the loud bassoon.

The bride hath paced into the hall,
Red as a rose is she:
Nodding their heads before her goes
The merry minstrelsy.

The Wedding-Guest he beat his breast,
Yet he cannot choose but hear;
And thus spake on that ancient man,
The bright-eyed Mariner.

And now the Storm-blast came, and he
Was tyrannous and strong:
He struck with his o'ertaking wings,
And chased us south along.

With sloping masts and dipping prow,
As who pursued with yell and blow
Still treads the shadow of his foe,
And forward bends his head,
The ship drove fast, loud roared the blast,
And southward aye we fled.

And now there came both mist and snow,
And it grew wondrous cold:
And ice, mast-high, came floating by,
As green as emerald.

And through the drifts the snowy clifts
Did send a dismal sheen:
Nor shapes of men nor beasts we ken –
The ice was all between.

The ice was here, the ice was there,
The ice was all around:
It cracked and growled, and roared and howled,
Like noises in a swound!

At length did cross an Albatross,
Thorough the fog it came;
As if it had been a Christian soul,
We hailed it in God's name.

It ate the food it ne'er had eat,
And round and round it flew.
The ice did split with a thunder-fit;
The helmsman steered us through!

And a good south wind sprung up behind;
The Albatross did follow,
And every day, for food or play,
Came to the mariners' hollo!

In mist or cloud, on mast or shroud,
It perched for vespers nine;
Whiles all the night, through fog-smoke white,
Glimmered the white moon-shine.

'God save thee, ancient Mariner!
From the fiends, that plague thee thus! –
Why look'st thou so?' – With my cross-bow
I shot the Albatross.

PART TWO

The sun now rose upon the right:
Out of the sea came he,
Still hid in mist, and on the left
Went down into the sea.

And the good south wind still blew behind,
But no sweet bird did follow,
Nor any day, for food or play,
Came to the mariners' hollo!

And I had done a hellish thing,
And it would work 'em woe:
For all averred, I had killed the bird
That made the breeze to blow.
'Ah wretch!' said they, 'the bird to slay,
That made the breeze to blow!'

Nor dim nor red, like God's own head,
The glorious Sun uprist:
Then all averred, I had killed the bird
That brought the fog and mist.
'Twas right,' said they, 'such birds to slay,
That bring the fog and mist.'

The fair breeze blew, the white foam flew,
The furrow followed free;
We were the first that ever burst
Into that silent sea.

Down dropt the breeze, the sails dropt down,
'Twas sad as sad could be;
And we did speak only to break
The silence of the sea!

All in a hot and copper sky,
The bloody Sun, at noon,
Right up above the mast did stand,
No bigger than the Moon.

Day after day, day after day,
We stuck, nor breath nor motion,
As idle as a painted ship
Upon a painted ocean.

Water, water, everywhere,
And all the boards did shrink;
Water, water, everywhere
Nor any drop to drink.

The very deep did rot: O Christ!
That ever this should be!
Yea, slimy things did crawl with legs
Upon the slimy sea.

About, about, in reel and rout
The death-fires danced at night;
The water, like a witch's oils,
Burnt green, and blue and white.

And some in dreams assurèd were
Of the Spirit that plagued us so;
Nine fathom deep he had followed us
From the land of mist and snow.

And every tongue, through utter drought,
Was withered at the root;
We could not speak, no more than if
We had been choked with soot.

Ah! well a-day! what evil looks
Had I from old and young!
Instead of the cross, the Albatross
About my neck was hung.

PART THREE

There passed a weary time. Each throat
Was parched, and glazed each eye.
A weary time! a weary time!
How glazed each weary eye,
When looking westward, I beheld
A something in the sky.

At first it seemed a little speck,
And then it seemed a mist;
It moved and moved, and took at last
A certain shape, I wist.

A speck, a mist, a shape, I wist!,
And still it neared and neared:
As if it dodged a water-sprite,
It plunged and tacked and veered.

With throats unslaked, with black lips baked,
We could not laugh nor wail;
Through utter drought all dumb we stood!
I bit my arm, I sucked the blood,
And cried, 'A sail! a sail!'

With throats unslaked, with black lips baked,
Agape they heard me call:
Gramercy! they for joy did grin,
And all at once their breath drew in,
As they were drinking all.

'See! see!' I cried 'she tacks no more!
Hither to work us weal;
Without a breeze, without a tide,
She steadies with upright keel!'

The western wave was all a-flame.
The day was well nigh done!
Almost upon the western wave
Rested the broad bright Sun;
When that strange shape drove suddenly
Betwixt us and the Sun.

And straight the Sun was flecked with bars,
(Heaven's Mother send us grace!)
As if through a dungeon-gate he peered
With broad and burning face.

Alas! (thought I, and my heart beat loud)
How fast she nears and nears!
Are those her sails that glance in the Sun,
Like restless gossameres?

Are those her ribs through which the Sun
Did peer, as through a grate?
And is that Woman all her crew?
Is that a Death? and are there two?
Is Death that Woman's mate?

Her lips were red, her looks were free,
Her locks were yellow as gold:
Her skin was as white as leprosy,
The Nightmare Life-in-Death was she,
Who thicks man's blood with cold.

The naked hulk alongside came,
And the twain were casting dice;
'The game is done! I've won! I've won!'
Quoth she, and whistles thrice.

The Sun's rim dips; the stars rush out:
At one stride comes the dark;
With far-heard whisper, o'er the sea,
Off shot the spectre-bark.

We listened and looked sideways up!
Fear at my heart, as at a cup,
My life-blood seemed to sip!
The stars were dim, and thick the night,
The steersman's face by his lamp gleamed white;
From the sails the dew did drip –
Till clomb above the eastern bar
The hornèd Moon, with one bright star
Within the nether tip.

One after one, by the star-dogged Moon,
Too quick for groan or sigh,
Each turned his face with a ghastly pang,
And cursed me with his eye.

Four times fifty living men,
(And I heard nor sigh nor groan),
With heavy thump, a lifeless lump,
They dropped down one by one.

The souls did from their bodies fly –
They fled to bliss or woe!
And every soul, it passed me by,
Like the whizz of my cross-bow!

PART FOUR

'I fear thee, ancient Mariner!
I fear thy skinny hand!
And thou art long, and lank, and brown,
As is the ribbed sea-sand.

'I fear thee and thy glittering eye,
And thy skinny hand, so brown.' –
Fear not, fear not, thou Wedding-Guest!
This body dropt not down.

Alone, alone, all, all alone,
Alone on a wide, wide sea!
And never a saint took pity on
My soul in agony.

The many men, so beautiful!
And they all dead did lie:
And a thousand thousand slimy things
Lived on; and so did I.

I looked upon the rotting sea,
And drew my eyes away;
I looked upon the rotting deck,
And there the dead men lay.

I looked to heaven, and tried to pray;
But or ever a prayer had gusht,
A wicked whisper came, and made
My heart as dry as dust.

I closed my lids, and kept them close,
And the balls like pulses beat;
For the sky and the sea, and the sea and the sky
Lay like a load on my weary eye,
And the dead were at my feet.

The cold sweat melted from their limbs,
Nor rot nor reek did they:
The look with which they looked on me
Had never passed away.

An orphan's curse would drag to hell
A spirit from on high;
But oh! more horrible than that
Is the curse in a dead man's eye!
Seven days, seven nights, I saw that curse,
And yet I could not die.

The moving Moon went up the sky,
And nowhere did abide:
Softly she was going up,
And a star or two beside –

Her beams bemocked the sultry main
Like April hoar-frost spread;
But where the ship's huge shadow lay,
The charmèd water burnt alway
A still and awful red.

Beyond the shadow of the ship,
I watched the water-snakes:
They moved in tracks of shining white,
And when they reared, the elfish light
Fell off in hoary flakes.

Within the shadow of the ship
I watched their rich attire:
Blue, glossy green, and velvet black,
They coiled and swam; and every track
Was a flash of golden fire.

O happy living things! no tongue
Their beauty might declare:
A spring of love gushed from my heart,
And I blessed them unaware:
Sure my kind saint took pity on me,
And I blessed them unaware.

The selfsame moment I could pray;
And from my neck so free
The Albatross fell off, and sank
Like lead into the sea.

PART FIVE

Oh sleep! it is a gentle thing,
Beloved from pole to pole!
To Mary Queen the praise be given!
She sent the gentle sleep from Heaven,
That slid into my soul.

The silly buckets on the deck,
That had so long remained,
I dreamt that they were filled with dew;
And when I awoke, it rained.

My lips were wet, my throat was cold,
My garments all were dank;
Sure I had drunken in my dreams,
And still my body drank.

I moved, and could not feel my limbs:
I was so light – almost
I thought that I had died in sleep,
And was a blessèd ghost.

And soon I heard a roaring wind:
It did not come anear;
But with its sound it shook the sails,
That were so thin and sere.

The upper air burst into life!
And a hundred fire-flags sheen,
To and fro they were hurried about!
And to and fro, and in and out,
The wan stars danced between.

And the coming wind did roar more loud,
And the sails did sigh like sedge;
And the rain poured down from one black cloud;
The Moon was at its edge.

The thick black cloud was cleft, and still
The Moon was at its side:
Like waters shot from some high crag,
The lightning fell with never a jag,
A river steep and wide.

The loud wind never reached the ship,
Yet now the ship moved on!
Beneath th lightning and the Moon
The dead men gave a groan.

They groaned, they stirred, they all uprose,
Nor spake, nor moved their eyes;
It had been strange, even in a dream,
To have seen those dead men rise.

The helmsman steered, the ship moved on;
Yet never a breeze up blew;
The mariners all 'gan work the ropes,
Where they were wont to do;
They raised their limbs like lifeless tools –
We were a ghastly crew.

The body of my brother's son
Stood by me, knee to knee:
The body and I pulled at one rope,
But he said nought to me.'

'I fear thee, ancient Mariner!'
Be calm, thou Wedding-Guest!
'Twas not those souls that fled in pain,
Which to their corses came again,
But a troop of spirits blest:

For when it dawned – they dropped their arms,
And clustered round the mast;
Sweet sounds rose slowly through their mouths,
And from their bodies passed.

Around, around, flew each sweet sound,
Then darted to the Sun;
Slowly the sounds came back again,
Now mixed, now one by one.

Sometimes a-dropping from the sky
I heard the skylark sing;
Sometimes all little birds that are,
How they seemed to fill the sea and air
With their sweet jargoning!

And now 'twas like all instruments,
Now like a lonely flute;
And now it is an angel's song,
That makes the heavens be mute.

It ceased; yet still the sails made on
A pleasant noise till noon,
A noise like of a hidden brook
In the leafy month of June,
That to the sleeping woods all night
Singeth a quiet tune.

Till noon we quietly sailed on,
Yet never a breeze did breathe:
Slowly and smoothly went the ship,
Moved onward from beneath.

Under the keel nine fathom deep,
From the land of mist and snow,
The Spirit slid: and it was he
That made the ship to go.
The sails at noon left off their tune,
And the ship stood still also.

The Sun, right up above the mast,
Had fixed her to the ocean:
But in a minute she 'gan stir,
With a short uneasy motion –
Backwards and forwards half her length
With a short uneasy motion.

Then like a pawing horse let go,
She made a sudden bound:
It flung the blood into my head,
And I fell down in a swound.

How long in that same fit I lay,
I have not to declare;
But ere my living life returned,
I heard, and in my soul discerned
Two voices in the air.

'Is it he?' quoth one, 'is this the man?
By Him who died on cross,
With his cruel bow he laid full low
The harmless Albatross.

The Spirit who bideth by himself
In the land of mist and snow,
He loved the bird that loved the man
Who shot him with his bow.'

The other was a softer voice,
As soft as honey-dew:
Quoth he, 'The man hath penance done,
And penance more will do.'

PART SIX

First Voice. 'But tell me, tell me! speak again,
Thy soft response renewing –
What makes that ship drive on so fast?
What is the ocean doing?'

Second Voice. 'Still as a slave before his lord,
The ocean hath no blast;
His great bright eye most silently
Up to the Moon is cast –

If he may know which way to go;
For she guides him smooth or grim.
See, brother, see! how graciously
She looketh down on him.'

First Voice. 'But why drives on that ship so fast,
Without or wave or wind?'

Second Voice. 'The air is cut away before,
And closes from behind.

Fly, brother, fly! more high, more high!
Or we shall be belated:
For slow and slow that ship will go,
When the Mariner's trance is abated.'

I woke, and we were sailing on
As in a gentle weather:
'Twas night, calm night, the Moon was high;
The dead men stood together.

All stood together on the deck,
For a charnel-dungeon fitter:
All fixed on me their stony eyes,
That in the Moon did glitter.

The pang, the curse, with which they died,
Had never passed away:
I could not draw my eyes from theirs,
Nor turn them up to pray.

And now this spell was snapt: once more
I view the ocean green,
And looked far north, yet little saw
Of what had else been seen –

Like one that on a lonesome road
Doth walk in fear and dread,
And having once turned round walks on,
And turns no more his head;
Because he knows, a frightful fiend
Doth close behind him tread.

But soon there breathed a wind on me,
Nor sound nor motion made:
Its path was not upon the sea,
In ripple or in shade.

It raised my hair, it fanned my cheek
Like a meadow-gale of spring –
It mingled strangely with my fears,
Yet it felt like a welcoming.

Swiftly, swiftly flew the ship,
Yet she sailed softly too:
Sweetly, sweetly blew the breeze –
On me alone it blew.

Oh! dream of joy! is this indeed
The lighthouse top I see?
Is this the hill? is this the kirk?
Is this mine own countree?

We drifted o'er the harbour-bar,
And I with sobs did pray –
'O let me be awake, my God!
Or let me sleep alway.'

The harbour-bay was clear as glass,
So smoothly it was strewn!
And on the bay the moonlight lay,
And the shadow of the Moon.

The rock shone bright, the kirk no less,
That stands above the rock:
The moonlight steeped in silentness
The steady weathercock.

And the bay was white with silent light,
Till rising from the same,
Full many shapes, that shadows were,
In crimson colours came.

A little distance from the prow
Those crimson shadows were:
I turned my eyes upon the deck –
O Christ! what saw I there!

Each corse lay flat, lifeless and flat,
And, by the holy rood!
A man all light, a seraph-man,
On every corse there stood.

This seraph-band, each waved his hand:
It was a heavenly sight!
They stood as signals to the land,
Each one a lovely light;

This seraph-band, each waved his hand,
No voice did they impart –
No voice; but oh! the silence sank
Like music on my heart.

But soon I heard the dash of oars,
I heard the Pilot's cheer;
My head was turned perforce away,
And I saw a boat appear.

The Pilot and the Pilot's boy,
I heard them coming fast:
Dear Lord in Heaven! it was a joy
The dead men could not blast.

I saw a third – I heard his voice:
It is the Hermit good!
He singeth loud his godly hymns
That he makes in the wood.
He'll shrieve my soul, he'll wash away
The Albatross's blood.

PART SEVEN

This Hermit good lives in that wood
Which slopes down to the sea.
How loudly his sweet voice he rears!
He loves to talk with marineres
That come from a far countree.

He kneels at morn, and noon, and eve –
He hath a cushion plump:
It is the moss that wholly hides
The rotted old oak-stump.

The skiff-boat neared: I heard them talk,
'Why, this is strange, I trow!
Where are those lights so many and fair,
That signal made but now?'

'Strange, by my faith!' the Hermit said –
'And they answered not our cheer!
The planks lok warped! and see those sails,
How thin they are and sere!
I never saw aught like to them,
Unless perchance it were

Brown skeletons of leaves that lag
My forest-brook along;
When the ivy-tod is heavy with snow,
And the owlet whoops, to the wolf below,
That eats the she-wolf's young.'

'Dear Lord! it hath a fiendish look'
(The Pilot made reply)
'I am a-feared.'–'Push on, push on!'
Said the Hermit cheerily.

The boat came closer to the ship,
But I nor spake nor stirred;
The boat came close beneath the ship,
And straight a sound was heard.

Under the water it rumbled on,
Still louder and more dread:
It reached the ship, it split the bay;
The ship went down like lead.

Stunned by that loud and dreadful sound,
Which sky and ocean smote,
Like one that hath been seven days drowned
My body lay afloat;
But swift as dreams, myself I found
Within the Pilot's boat.

Upon the whirl, where sank the ship,
The boat spun round and round;
And all was still, save that the hill
Was telling of the sound.

I moved my lips – the Pilot shrieked
And fell down in a fit;
The holy Hermit raised his eyes,
And prayed where he did sit.

I took the oars: the Pilot's boy,
Who now doth crazy go,
Laughed loud and long, and all the while
His eyes went to and fro.
'Ha! ha!' quoth he, 'full plain I see,
The Devil knows how to row.'

And now, all in my own countree,
I stood on the firm land!
The Hermit stepped forth from the boat,
And scarcely he could stand.

'O shrieve me, shrieve me, holy man!'
The Hermit crossed his brow.
'Say quick,' quoth he, 'I bid thee say –
What manner of man art thou?'

Forthwith this frame of mine was wrenched
With a woful agony,
Which forced me to begin my tale;
And then it left me free.

Since then, at an uncertain hour,
That agony returns:
And till my ghastly tale is told,
This heart within me burns.

I pass, like night, from land to land;
I have strange power of speech;
That moment that his face I see,
I know the man that must hear me:
To him my tale I teach.

What loud uproar bursts from that door!
The wedding-guests are there:
But in the garden-bower the bride
And bridesmaids singing are:
And hark, the little vesper bell,
Which biddeth me to prayer!

O Wedding-Guest! this soul hath been
Alone on a wide, wide sea;
So lonely 'twas, that God Himself
Scarce seemèd there to be.

O sweeter than the marriage-feast,
'Tis sweeter far to me,
To walk together to the kirk
With a goodly company!–

To walk together to the kirk,
And all together pray,
While each to his great Father bends,
Old men, and babes, and loving friends,
And youths and maidens gay!

Farewell, farewell! but this I tell
To thee, thou Wedding-Guest!
He prayeth well, who loveth well
Both man and bird and beast.

He prayeth best, who loveth best
All things both great and small;
For the dear God who loveth us,
He made and loveth all.

The Mariner, whose eye is bright,
Whose beard with age is hoar,
Is gone: and now the Wedding-Guest
Turned from the bridegroom's door.

He went like one that hath been stunned,
And is of sense forlorn:
A sadder and a wiser man,
He rose the morrow morn.

Samuel Taylor Coleridge

Storm off the Suffolk coast

Darkness begins to reign; the louder wind
Appals the weak and awes the firmer mind;
But frights not him, whom evening and the spray
In part conceal - yon Prowler on his way:
Lo! he has something seen; he runs apace,
As if he fear'd companion in the chase;
He sees his prize, and now he turns again,
Slowly and sorrowing - 'Was your search in vain?'
Gruffly he answers, ''Tis a sorry sight!
'A seaman's body: there'll be more tonight!'
Hark! to those sounds! they're from distress at sea:
How quick they come! What terrors may there be!
Yes, 'tis a driven vessel: I discern
Lights, signs of terror, gleaming from the stern;
Others behold them too, and from the town
In various parties seamen hurry down;
Their wives pursue, and damsels urged by dread,
Lest men so dear be into danger led;
Their head the gown has hooded, and their call
In this sad night is piercing like the squall;
They feel their kinds of power, and when they meet,
Chide, fondle, weep, dare, threaten, or entreat.
See one poor girl, all terror and alarm,
Has fondly seized upon her lover's arm;
'Thou shalt not venture;' and he answers 'No!
'I will not' - still she cries, 'Thou shalt not go.'
No need of this; not here the stoutest boat
Can through such breakers, o'er such billows float,
Yet may they view these lights upon the beach,
Which yield them hope, whom help can never reach.
From parted clouds the moon her radiance throws
On the wild waves, and all the danger shows;

But shows them beaming in her shining vest,
Terrific splendour! gloom in glory dress'd!
This for a moment, and then clouds again
Hide every beam, and fear and darkness reign.
    But hear we now those sounds? Do lights appear?
I see them not! the storm alone I hear:
And lo! the sailors homeward take their way;
Man must endure – let us submit and pray.

George Crabbe
from 'The Borough'

Relic

I found this jawbone at the sea's edge:
There, crabs, dogfish, broken by the breakers or tossed
To flap for half an hour and turn to a crust
Continue the beginning. The deeps are cold:
In that darkness camaraderie does not hold:
Nothing touches but, clutching, devours. And the jaws,
Before they are satisfied or their stretched purpose
Slacken, go down jaws; go gnawn bare. Jaws
Eat and are finished and the jawbone comes to the beach:
This is the sea's achievement; with shells,
Vertebrae, claws, carapaces, skulls.

Time in the sea eats its tail, thrives, casts these
Indigestibles, the spars of purposes
That failed far from the surface. None grow rich
In the sea. This curved jawbone did not laugh
But gripped, gripped and is now a cenotaph.

Ted Hughes

Blow, bugle, blow

The splendour falls on castle walls
And snowy summits old in story:
The long light shakes across the lakes,
And the wild cataract leaps in glory.
Blow, bugle, blow, set the wild echoes flying,
Blow, bugle; answer, echoes, dying, dying, dying.

O hark, O hear! how thin and clear,
And thinner, clearer, farther going!
O sweet and far from cliff and scar
The horns of Elfland faintly blowing!
Blow, let us hear the purple glens replying:
Blow, bugle; answer, echoes, dying, dying, dying.

O love, they die in yon rich sky,
They faint on hill or field or river:
Our echoes roll from soul to soul,
And grow for ever and for ever.
Blow, bugle, blow, set the wild echoes flying,
And answer, echoes, answer, dying, dying, dying.

Lord Tennyson

My brother was a pilot

My brother was a pilot,
He received a card one day,
He packed his belongings in a box
And southward took his way.

My brother is a conqueror,
Our people is short of space
And to gain more territory is
An ancient dream of the race.

The space that my brother conquered
Lies in the Guadarrama massif;
Its length is six feet, two inches,
Its depth four feet and a half.

Bertolt Brecht
translated by Michael Hamburger

Five minutes after the air raid

In Pilsen,
Twenty-six Station Road,
she climbed to the Third Floor
up stairs which were all that was left
of the whole house,
she opened her door
full on to the sky,
stood gaping over the edge.

For this was the place
the world ended.

Then
she locked up carefully
lest someone steal
Sirius
or Aldebaran
from her kitchen,

went back downstairs
and settled herself
to wait
for the house to rise again
and for her husband to rise from the ashes
and for her children's hands and feet to be stuck
back in place.

In the morning they found her
still as stone,
sparrows pecking her hands.

Miroslav Holub
translated by Ian Milner and George Theiner

War chant

The white man has brought his war to the beach.
If they look for bloody battle, they shall have it.
The amazons gather round their king and swear:
With our teeth we shall tear their throats.
Our fire drives them back to the men.
Their priest falls victim to our war.
With their teeth the amazons tore his throat.
Oil palms are felled and come crashing down.
The white man's boat is seized in the lagoon.

Traditional African song,
from the Fon people in Dahomey

Lament of the frontier guard

By the North Gate, the wind blows full of sand,
Lonely from the beginning of time until now!
Trees fall, the grass goes yellow with autumn.
I climb the towers and towers
    to watch out the barbarous land:
Desolate castle, the sky, the wide desert.
There is no wall left to this village.
Bones white with a thousand frosts,
High heaps, covered with trees and grass;
Who brought this to pass?
Who has brought the flaming imperial anger?
Who has brought the army with drums and with kettle-drums?
Barbarous kings.
A gracious spring, turned to blood-ravenous autumn,
A turmoil of wars-men, spread over the middle kingdom,
Three hundred and sixty thousand,
And sorrow, sorrow like rain.
Sorrow to go, and sorrow, sorrow returning.
Desolate, desolate fields,
And no children of warfare upon them,
    No longer the men for offence and defence.
Ah, how shall you know the dreary sorrow at the North Gate,
With Rihaku's name forgotten,
And we guardsmen fed to the tigers.

Rihaku, an eighteenth-century Chinese writer
translated by Ezra Pound

The companion

She was sitting on the rough embankment,
her cape too big for her tied on slapdash
over an odd little hat with a bobble on it,
her eyes brimming with tears of hopelessness.
An occasional butterfly floated down
fluttering warm wings on to the rails.
The clinkers underfoot were deep lilac.
We got cut off from our grandmothers
while the Germans were dive-bombing the train.
Katya was her name. She was nine.
I'd no idea what I could do about her,
but doubt quickly dissolved to certainty:
I'd have to take this thing under my wing;
– girls were in some sense of the word human,
a human being couldn't just be left.
The droning in the air and the explosions
receded farther into the distance,
I touched the little girl on her elbow.
'Come on. Do you hear? What are you waiting for?'
The world was big and we were not big,
and it was tough for us to walk across it.
She had galoshes on and felt boots,
I had a pair of second-hand boots.
We forded streams and tramped across the forest;
each of my feet at every step it took
taking a smaller step inside the boot.
The child was feeble, I was certain of it.
'Boo-hoo,' she'd say. 'I'm tired,' she'd say.
She'd tire in no time I was certain of it,
but as things turned out it was me who tired.
I growled I wasn't going any further
and sat down suddenly beside the fence.

'What's the matter with you?' she said.
'Don't be so stupid! Put grass in your boots.
Do you want to eat something? Why won't you talk?
Hold this tin, this is crab.
We'll have refreshments. You small boys,
you're always pretending to be brave.'
Then out I went across the prickly stubble
marching beside her in a few minutes.
Masculine pride was muttering in my mind:
I scraped together strength and I held out
for fear of what she'd say. I even whistled.
Grass was sticking out from my tattered boots.
So on and on
we walked without thinking of rest
passing craters, passing fire,
under the rocking sky of '41
tottering crazy on its smoking columns.

Yevgeny Yevtushenko

The battle of Stamford Bridge

Haste thee, Harold, haste thee North!
    Norway ships in Humber crowd.
Tall Hardrada, Sigurd's son,
For thy ruin this hath done –
    England for his own hath vowed.

'The earls have fought, the earls are fled.
  From Tyne to Ouse the homesteads flame.
York behind her battered wall
Waits the instant of her fall
  And the shame of England's name.

'Traitor Tosti's banner streams
  With the invading Raven's wing;
Black the land and red the skies
When Northumbria bleeds and cries
  For thy vengeance, England's King!'

Since that frighted summons flew
  Not twelve suns have sprung and set.
Northward marching night and day
Has King Harold kept his way.
  The hour is come; the hosts are met.

Morn through thin September mist
  Flames on moving helm and man.
On either side of Derwent's banks
Are the Northmen's shielded ranks;
  But silent stays the English van.

A rider to Earl Tosti comes:
  'Turn thee, Tosti, to thy kin!
Harold thy brother brings thee sign
All Northumbria shall be thine.
  Make thy peace, ere the fray begin!'

'And if I turn me to my kin,
  And if I stay the Northmen's hand,
What will Harold give to my friend this day?
To Norway's king what price will he pay
  Out of this English land?'

That rider laughed a mighty laugh.
    'Six full feet of English soil!
Or, since he is taller than the most,
Seven feet shall he have to boast;
    This Harold gives for Norway's spoil.'

'What rider was he that spoke thee fair?'
    Harold Hardrada to Tosti cried.
'It was Harold of England spoke me fair;
But now of his bane let him beware.
    Set on, set on! we will break his pride.'

Sudden arrows flashed and flew,
    Dark lines of English leapt and rushed
With sound of storm that stung like hail,
And steel rang sharp on supple mail
    With thrust that pierced and blow that crushed.

And sullenly back in a fierce amaze
    The Northmen gave to the river side.
The main of their host on the further shore
Could help them nothing, pressed so sore.
    In the ooze they fought, in the wave they died.

On a narrow bridge alone one man
    The English mass and fury stays.
The spears press close, the timber cracks
But high he swings his dreadful axe,
    With every stroke a life he slays;

But pierced at last from the stream below
    He falls: the Northmen break and shout.
Forward they hurl in wild onset;
But as struggling fish in a mighty net
    The English hem them round about.

Now Norway's king grew battle-mad,
    Mad with joy of his strength he smote.
But as he hewed his battle-path,
And heaped the dead men for a swath,
    An arrow clove him through the throat.

Where he slaughtered, red he fell.
    O then was Norway's hope undone,
Doomed men were they that fought in vain,
Hardrada slain, and Tosti slain!
    The field was lost, the field was won.

York this night rings all her bells.
    Harold feasts within her halls.
The Captains lift their wine-cups.– Hark!
What hoofs come thudding through the dark
    And sudden stop? What silence falls?

Spent with riding staggers in
    One who cries: 'Fell news I bring.
Duke William has o'erpast the sea.
His host is camped at Pevensey.
    Save us, save England now, O King!'

Woe to Harold! Twice 'tis not
    His to conquer and to save.
Well he knows the lot is cast.
England claims him to the last.
    South he marches to his grave.

Laurence Binyon

An incident of the French camp

You know, we French stormed Ratisbon:
    A mile or so away,
On a little mound, Napoleon
    Stood on our storming-day;
With neck out-thrust, you fancy how,
    Legs wide, arms locked behind,
As if to balance the prone brow
    Oppressive with its mind.

Just as perhaps he mused, 'My plans
    That soar, to earth may fall,
Let once my army-leader Lannes
    Waver at yonder wall,'–
Out 'twixt the battery-smokes there flew
    A rider, bound on bound
Full galloping; nor bridle drew
    Until he reached the mound.

Then off there flung in smiling joy,
    And held himself erect
By just his horse's mane, a boy:
    You hardly could suspect–
(So tight he kept his lips compressed,
    Scarce any blood came through)
You looked twice ere you saw his breast
    Was all but shot in two.

'Well,' cried he, 'Emperor, by God's grace
    We've got you Ratisbon!
The Marshal's in the market-place,
    And you'll be there anon
To see your flag-bird flap his vans
    Where I, to heart's desire,
Perched him!' The Chief's eye flashed; his plans
    Soared up again like fire.

The Chief's eye flashed; but presently
    Softened itself, as sheathes
A film the mother-eagle's eye
    When her bruised eaglet breathes;
'You're wounded!' 'Nay,' the soldier's pride
    Touched to the quick, he said:
'I'm killed, Sire!' And, his chief beside,
    Smiling the boy fell dead.

Robert Browning

At fifteen I went with the army

At fifteen I went with the army,
At fourscore I came home.
On the way I met a man from the village,
I asked him who there was at home.
'That over there is your house,
All covered over with trees and bushes.'
Rabbits had run in at the dog-hole,
Pheasants flew down from the beams of the roof.
In the courtyard was growing some wild grain;
        the well, some wild mallows.

I'll boil the grain and make porridge,
I'll pluck the mallows and make soup.
Soup and porridge are both cooked,
But there is no one to eat them with.
I went out and looked towards the east,
While tears fell and wetted my clothes.

Unknown Chinese poet,
translated by Arthur Waley

Death of an aircraft

AN INCIDENT OF THE CRETAN CAMPAIGN 1941

One day on our village in the month of July
An aeroplane sank from the sea of the sky,
　　White as a whale it smashed on the shore
　　Bleeding oil and petrol all over the floor.

The Germans advanced in the vertical heat
To save the dead plane from the people of Crete,
　　And round the glass wreck in a circus of snow
　　Set seven mechanical sentries to go.

Seven stalking spiders about the sharp sun
Clicking like clockwork and each with a gun,
　　But at *Come to the Cookhouse* they wheeled about
　　And sat down to sausages and sauerkraut.

Down from the mountain burning so brown
Wriggled three heroes from Kastelo town,
　　Deep in the sand they silently sank
　　And each struck a match for a petrol-tank.

Up went the plane in a feather of fire
As the bubbling boys began to retire
    And, grey in the guardhouse, seven Berliners
    Lost their stripes as well as their dinners.

Down in the village, at murder-stations,
The Germans fell in friends and relations:
    But not a Kastelian snapped an eye
    As he spat in the air and prepared to die.

Not a Kastelian whispered a word
Dressed with the dust to be massacred,
    And squinted up at the sky with a frown
    As three bubbly boys came walking down.

One was sent to the county gaol
Too young for bullets if not for bail,
    But the other two were in prime condition
    To take on a load of ammunition.

In Archontiki they stood in the weather
Naked, hungry, chained together:
    Stark as the stones in the market-place,
    Under the eye of the populace.

Their irons unlocked as their naked hearts
They faced the squad and their funeral-carts.
    The Captain cried, 'B fore you're away
    Is there any last word you'd like to say?'

'I want no words,' said one, 'with my lead,
Only some water to cool my head.'
    'Water,' the other said, 'is all very fine
    But I'll be taking a glass of wine.

'A glass of wine for the afternoon
With permission to sing a signature-tune!'
    And he ran the *raki* down his throat
    And took a deep breath for the leading note.

But before the squad could shoot or say
Like the impala he leapt away
    Over the rifles, under the biers,
    The bullets rattling round his ears.

'Run!' they cried to the boy of stone
Who now stood there in the street alone,
    But, 'Rather than bring revenge on your head
    It is better for me to die,' he said.

The soldiers turned their machine-guns round
And shot him down with a dreadful sound
    Scrubbed his face with perpetual dark
    And rubbed it out like a pencil mark.

But his comrade slept in the olive tree
And sailed by night on the gnawing sea,
    The soldier's silver shilling earned
    And, armed like an archangel, returned.

Charles Causley

O Captain! My Captain!

O Captain! my Captain! our fearful trip is done!
The ship has weathered every wrack,
                                        the prize we sought is won.
The port is near, the bells I hear,
                                        the people all exulting,
While follow eyes the steady keel,
                                        the vessel grim and daring.
    But, O heart! heart! heart!
        Leave you not the little spot
            Where on the deck my Captain lies,
                Fallen cold and dead.

O Captain! my Captain! rise up and hear the bells;
Rise up – for you the flag is flung –
for you the bugle trills,
For you bouquets and ribbon'd wreaths –
for you the shores a-crowding,
For you they call, the swaying mass,
their eager faces turning.
Here, Captain, dear father!
This arm I push beneath you.
It is some dream that on the deck
You've fallen cold and dead.

My Captain does not answer, his lips are pale and still,
My father does not feel my arm,
he has no pulse nor will;
The ship is anchor'd safe and sound,
its voyage closed and done,
From fearful trip the victor ship
comes in with object won;
Exult, O shores! and ring, O bells!
But I, with silent tread,
Walk the spot my Captain lies,
Fallen cold and dead.

Walt Whitman

Children's crusade 1939

In 'thirty-nine, in Poland
a bloody battle took place,
turning many a town and village
into a wilderness.

The sister lost her brother,
the wife her husband in war,
the child between fire and rubble
could find his parents no more.

From Poland no news was forthcoming
neither letter nor printed word,
but in all the Eastern countries
a curious tale can be heard.

Snow fell when they told one another
this tale in an Eastern town
of a children's crusade that started
in Poland, in 'thirty-nine.

Along the highroads in squadrons
there hungry children tripped,
and on their way picked up others
in villages gutted and stripped.

They wanted to flee from the fighting
so that the nightmare would cease
and one day at last they'd arrive in
a country where there was peace.

They had a little leader
who was their prop and stay.
This leader had one great worry:
he did not know the way.

A girl of eleven carried
a toddler of four without cease,
lacking nothing that makes a mother
but a country where there was peace.

A little Jewish boy marched in the troop,
with velvet collar and cuff,
he was used to the whitest of bread
and he fought bravely enough.

And two brothers joined this army,
each a mighty strategist,
these took an empty cottage by storm
with nothing but rain to resist.

And a lean grey fellow walked there,
by the roadside, in isolation,
and bore the burden of terrible guilt:
he came from a Nazi legation.

There was a musician among them
who in a shelled village found a drum one day
and was not allowed to strike it,
so as not to give them away.

And there was also a dog,
caught for the knife at the start,
yet later kept on as an eater
because no one had the heart.

And they had a school there also,
and a small teacher who knew how to yell,
and a pupil against the wall of a shot-up tank
as far as peac . . . learned to spell.

And there was a concert too:
by a roaring winter stream one lad
was allowed to beat the drum,
but no one heard him. Too bad.

And there was a love affair.
She was twelve, he was fifteen.
In a secluded courtyard
she combed his hair.

This love could not last long,
too cold the weather came on.
How can the little tree flower
with so much snow coming down?

And there was a war as well,
for there was another crowd beside this
and the war only came to an end
because it was meaningless.

But when the war still raged
around a shelled pointman's hut,
suddenly, so they say, one party
found their food supply had been cut.

And when the other heard this, they sent
a man to relieve their plight
with a sack of potatoes, because
without food one cannot fight.

There was a trial too,
with a pair of candles for light,
and after much painful examining
the judge was found guilty that night.

And a funeral too: of a boy
with velvet on collar and wrist;
it was two Poles and two Germans
carried him to his rest.

Protestant, Catholic and Nazi were there
when his body to earth they were giving,
and at the end a little Socialist spoke
of the future of the living.

So there was faith and hope,
only no meat and no bread,
and let no man blame them if they stole a few things
when he offered no board or bed.

And let no man blame the needy man
who offered no bread or rice,
for with fifty to feed it's a matter
of flour, not self-sacrifice.

They made for the south in the main.
The south is where the sun
at midday, twelve o'clock sharp
lies straight in front of one.

True, they found a soldier
who wounded on fir-needles lay.
They nursed him for seven days
so he could show them the way.

He told them: To Bilgoray!
Delirious, surely, far gone,
and he died on the eighth day.
They buried him too, and moved on.

And there were sign-posts also,
though snow rubbed the writing out;
only they'd ceased to point the way,
having been turned about.

This was not for a practical joke,
but on a military ground,
and when they looked for Bilgoray
the place was not to be found.

They stood around their leader
who looked up at the snowy air
and, extending his little hand,
said, it must be over there.

Once, at night, they saw a fire,
but better not go, they decided.
Once three tanks rolled past them,
each with people inside it.

Once, too, they came to a city,
and skirted it, well out of sight;
till they'd left it well behind them
they only marched on at night.

In what used to be South-East Poland
when snow swept the landscape clean
that army of fifty-five children
was last seen.

If I close my eyes and try,
I can see them trudge on
from one shell-blasted homestead
to another shell-blasted one.

Above them, in the cloudy spaces,
I see new long trains progress,
painfully trudging in the cold wind's face,
homeless, directionless.

Looking for the country at peace,
without fire and thunder's blast,
not like that from which they have come;
and the train grows vast.

And soon in the flickering half-light
no longer the same it seemed:
other little faces I saw,
Spanish, French, yellow ones gleamed.

That January, in Poland
a stray dog was caught;
hanging from its lean neck
a cardboard notice it brought.

It read: please come and help us!
We no longer know the way.
There are fifty-five of us.
The dog won't lead you astray.

Don't shoot him dead.
Only he knows the place.
With him
our very last hope you'd efface.

The writing was in a child's hand.
By farmers it was read.
Since then a year and a half have passed.
The dog, who was starving, is dead.

Bertolt Brecht
translated by Michael Hamburger

The old cloak

This winter's weather it waxeth cold,
    And frost it freezeth on every hill,
And Boreas blows his blast so bold
    That all our cattle are like to spill.[1]
Bell, my wife, she loves no strife;
    She said unto me quietly,
Rise up, and save cow Crumbock's life!
    Man, put thine old cloak about thee!

HE: 'O Bell, my wife, who dost thou flyte?[2]
    Thou kens my cloak is very thin:
It is so bare and overworn,
    A crickè thereon cannot rin.
Then I'll no longer borrow nor lend;
    For once I'll new apparell'd be;
Tomorrow I'll to town and spend;
    For I'll have a new cloak about me.'

SHE: 'Cow Crumbock is a very good cow:
    She has been always true to the pail;
She has helped us to butter and cheese, I trow,
    And other things she will not fail.
I would be loth to see her pine.
    Good husband, counsel take of me:
It is not for us to go so fine –
    Man, take thine old cloak about thee!'

HE: 'My cloak it was a very good cloak,
    It hath been always true to the wear;
But now it is not worth a groat:
    I have had it four and forty year.

[1] to waste away
[2] grumble

Sometimes it was of cloth in grain:[1]
'Tis now but a sigh clout,[2] as you may see:
It will neither hold out wind nor rain;
And I'll have a new cloak about me.'

SHE: 'It is four and forty years ago
Sine the one of us the other did ken;
And we have had betwixt us two,
Of children either nine or ten:
We have brought them up to women and men:
In the fear of God I trow they be:
And why wilt thou thyself misken?[3]
Man, take thine old cloak about thee!'

HE: 'O Bell, my wife, why dost thou flyte?
Now is now, and then was then:
Seek now all the world throughout,
Thou kens not clowns from gentlemen:
They are clad in black, green, yellow and blue,
So far above their own degree.
Once in my life I'll take a view;
For I'll have a new cloak about me.'

SHE: 'King Stephen was a worthy peer;
His breeches cost him but a crown;
He held them sixpence all too dear,
Therefore he called the tailor lown.
He was a king and wore the crown,
And thou'se but of a low degree:
It's pride that puts this country down:
Man, take thy old cloak about thee!'

[1] dyed with fast colour
[2] a poor piece of cloth
[3] deceive

Bell, my wife, she loves not strife,
Yet she will lead me, if she can;
And to maintain an easy life
I oft must yield, though I'm good-man.
It's not for a man with a woman to threap,[1]
Unless he first give o'er the plea:
As we began, so will we keep,
And I'll take my old cloak about me.

Not known

The diverting history of John Gilpin

Showing how he went farther than he intended, and came safe home again

John Gilpin was a citizen
Of credit and renown,
A train-band captain eke was he
Of famous London Town.

John Gilpin's spouse said to her dear –
'Though wedded we have been
These twice ten tedious years, yet we
No holiday have seen.

'Tomorrow is our wedding-day,
And we will then repair
Unto the Bell at Edmonton,
All in a chaise and pair.

[1] argue

'My sister, and my sister's child,
Myself, and children three,
Will fill the chaise; so you must ride
On horseback after we.'

He soon replied – 'I do admire
Of womankind but one,
And you are she, my dearest dear,
Therefore it shall be done.

'I am a linen-draper bold,
As all the world doth know,
And my good friend the calender[1]
Will lend his horse to go.'

Quoth Mrs Gilpin – 'That's well said;
And, for that wine is dear,
We will be furnished with our own,
Which is both bright and clear.'

John Gilpin kissed his loving wife;
O'erjoyed was he to find
That, though on pleasure she was bent,
She had a frugal mind.

The morning came, the chaise was brought,
But yet was not allowed
To drive up to the door, lest all
Should say that she was proud.

So three doors off the chaise was stayed,
Where they did all get in;
Six precious souls, and all agog
To dash through thick and thin!

[1] maker of cloth

Smack went the whip, round went the wheels,
    Were never folk so glad,
The stones did rattle underneath,
    As if Cheapside were mad.

John Gilpin at his horse's side
    Seized fast the flowing mane,
And up he got, in haste to ride,
    But soon came down again;

For saddle-tree scarce reached had he,
    His journey to begin,
When, turning round his head, he saw
    Three customers come in.

So down he came; for loss of time,
    Although it grieved him sore,
Yet loss of pence, full well he knew,
    Would trouble him much more.

'Twas long before the customers
    Were suited to their mind,
When Betty screaming came downstairs –
    'The wine is left behind!'

'Good lack!' quoth he – 'yet bring it me,
    My leathern belt likewise,
In which I bear my trusty sword
    When I do exercise.'

Now mistress Gilpin (careful soul!)
    Had two stone bottles found,
To hold the liquor that she loved,
    And keep it safe and sound.

Each bottle had a curling ear,
    Through which the belt he drew,
And hung a bottle on each side,
    To make his balance true.

Then, over all, that he might be
    Equipped from top to toe,
His long red cloak, well brushed and neat,
    He manfully did throw.

Now see him mounted once again
    Upon his nimble steed,
Full slowly pacing o'er the stones,
    With caution and good heed!

But, finding soon a smoother road
    Beneath his well-shod feet,
The snorting beast began to trot,
    Which galled him in his seat.

So, 'Fair and softly,' John he cried,
    But John he cried in vain;
That trot became a gallop soon,
    In spite of curb and rein.

So stooping down, as needs he must
    Who cannot sit upright,
He grasped the mane with both his hands,
    And eke with all his might.

His horse, who never in that sort
    Had handled been before,
What thing upon his back had got
    Did wonder more and more.

Away went Gilpin, neck or nought;
    Away went hat and wig! –
He little dreamt, when he set out,
    Of running such a rig!

The wind did blow, the cloak did fly
    Like streamer long and gay,
Till, loop and button failing both,
    At last it flew away.

Then might all people well discern
    The bottles he had slung;
A bottle swinging at each side,
    As hath been said or sung.

The dogs did bark, the children screamed,
    Up flew the windows all;
And ev'ry soul cried out – 'Well done!'
    As loud as he could bawl.

Away went Gilpin – Who but he?
    His fame soon spread around –
'He carries weight!' 'He rides a race!'
'Tis for a thousand pound!'

And still, as fast as he drew near,
    'Twas wonderful to view
How in a trice the turnpike-men
    Their gates wide open threw.

And now, as he went bowing down
    His reeking head full low,
The bottles twain behind his back
    Were shattered at a blow.

Down ran the wine into the road,
    Most piteous to be seen,
Which made his horse's flanks to smoke
    As they had basted been.

But still he seemed to carry weight,
    With leathern girdle braced;
For all might see the bottle-necks
    Still dangling at his waist.

Thus all through merry Islington
  These gambols he did play,
Until he came unto the Wash[1]
  Of Edmonton so gay.

And there he threw the wash[2] about
  On both sides of the way,
Just like unto a trundling mop,
  Or a wild goose at play.

At Edmonton his loving wife
  From the balcony spied
Her tender husband, wond'ring much
  To see how he did ride.

'Stop, stop, John Gilpin! - Here's the house' -
  They all at once did cry;
'The dinner waits, and we are tired.'
  Said Gilpin - 'So am I!'

But yet his horse was not a whit
  Inclined to tarry there;
For why? - his owner had a house
  Full ten miles off, at Ware.

So like an arrow swift he flew,
  Shot by an archer strong;
So did he fly - which brings me to
  The middle of my song.

Away went Gilpin, out of breath,
  And sore against his will,
Till at his friend the calender's
  His horse at last stood still.

[1] a low-lying stretch of land
[2] pools of water lying on the marshy ground

The calender, amazed to see
His neighbour in such trim,
Laid down his pipe, flew to the gate,
And thus accosted him:-

'What news? what news? your tidings tell;
Tell me you must and shall -
Say why bare-headed you are come,
Or why you come at all?'

Now Gilpin had a pleasant wit,
And loved a timely joke;
And thus unto the calender
In merry guise he spoke:-

'I came because your horse would come;
And, if I well forebode,
My hat and wig will soon be here -
They are upon the road.'

The calender, right glad to find
His friend in merry pin,
Returned him not a single word,
But to the house went in;

Whence straight he came with hat and wig;
A wig that flowed behind,
A hat not much the worse for wear,
Each comely in its kind.

He held them up, and, in his turn,
Thus showed his ready wit -
'My head is twice as big as yours,
They therefore needs must fit.

'But let me scrape the dirt away
That hangs upon your face;
And stop and eat, for well you may
Be in a hungry case.'

Said John – 'It is my wedding-day,
    And all the world would stare,
If wife should dine at Edmonton
    And I should dine at Ware!'

So turning to his horse, he said –
    'I am in haste to dine;
'Twas for your pleasure you came here,
    You shall go back for mine.'

Ah, luckless speech, and bootless boast!
    For which he paid full dear;
For, while he spake, a braying ass
    Did sing most loud and clear;

Whereat his horse did snort, as he
    Had heard a lion roar,
And galloped off with all his might,
    As he had done before.

Away went Gilpin, and away
    Went Gilpin's hat and wig!
He lost them sooner than at first –
    For why? – they were too big!

Now, mistress Gilpin, when she saw
    Her husband posting down
Into the country far away,
    She pulled out half a crown;

And thus unto the youth she said
    That drove them to the Bell –
'This shall be yours when you bring back
    My husband safe and well.'

The youth did ride, and soon did meet
    John coming back amain;
Whom in a trice he tried to stop
    By catching at his rein;

But, not performing what he meant,
    And gladly would have done,
The frighted steed he frighted more,
    And made him faster run.

Away went Gilpin, and away
    Went post-boy at his heels!-
The post-boy's horse right glad to miss
    The lumb'ring of the wheels.

Six gentlemen upon the road,
    Thus seeing Gilpin fly,
With post-boy scamp'ring in the rear,
    They raised the hue and cry:

'Stop thief! stop thief! - a highwayman!'
    Not one of them was mute;
And all and each that passed that way
    Did join in the pursuit.

And now the turnpike gates again
    Flew open in short space;
The toll-men thinking, as before,
    That Gilpin rode a race.

And so he did - and won it too! -
    For he got first to town;
Nor stopped till where he had got up
    He did again get down.

Now let us sing - Long live the king,
    And Gilpin long live he;
And, when he next doth ride abroad,
    May I be there to see!

William Cowper

Sir Smasham Uppe

'Good afternoon, Sir Smasham Uppe!
We're having tea: do take a cup!
Sugar and milk? Now let me see –
Two lumps, I think? . . . Good gracious me!
The silly thing slipped off your knee!
Pray don't apologise, old chap:
A very trivial mishap!
So clumsy of you? How absurd!
My dear Sir Smasham, not a word!

'Now do sit down and have another,
And tell us all about your brother –
You know, the one who broke his head.
Is the poor fellow still in bed? –
A chair – allow me, sir! . . . Great Scott!
That *was* a nasty smash! Eh, what?
Oh, not at all: the chair was old –
Queen Anne, or so we have been told.
We've got at least a dozen more:
Just leave the pieces on the floor.
I want you to admire our view:
Come nearer to the window, do;
And look how beautiful . . . Tut, tut!
You didn't see that it was shut?
I hope you are not badly cut!
Not hurt? A fortunate escape!
Amazing! Not a single scrape!

'And now, if you have finished tea,
I fancy you might like to see
A little thing or two I've got.
That china plate? Yes, worth a lot:
A beauty too . . . Ah, there it goes!
I trust it didn't hurt your toes?
Your elbow brushed it off the shelf?
Of course: I've done the same myself.
And now, my dear Sir Smasham - oh,
You surely don't intend to go?
You *must* be off? Well, come again.
So glad you're fond of porcelain!'

E V Rieu

Domestic asides

or *Truth in parentheses*

'I really take it very kind,
    This visit, Mrs Skinner!
I have not seen you such an age -
    (The wretch has come to dinner!)

'Your daughters, too, what loves of girls -
    What heads for painters' easels!
Come here and kiss the infant, dears -
    (And give it perhaps the measles!)

'Your charming boys I see are home
    From Reverend Mr Russell's;
'Twas very kind to bring them both -
    (What boots for my new Brussels!)

'What! little Clara left at home?
Well now I call that shabby:
I should have loved to kiss her so –
(A flabby, dabby, babby!)

'And Mr S., I hope he's well,
Ah! though he lives so handy,
He never now drops in to sup –
(The better for our brandy!)

'Come, take a seat – I long to hear
About Matilda's marriage;
You're come of course to spend the day!
(Thank Heaven, I hear the carriage!)

'What! must you go? next time I hope
You'll give me longer measure;
Nay – I shall see you down the stairs –
(With most uncommon pleasure!)

'Good-bye! good-bye! remember all,
Next time you'll take your dinners!
(Now, David, mind I'm not at home
In future to the Skinners!)'

Thomas Hood

The wee cooper o' Fife

There was a wee cooper who lived in Fife,
Nickity, nackity, noo, noo, noo.
And he has gotten a gentle wife.
Hey Willie Wallacky, how John Dougall,
Alane, quo' Rushety, roue, roue, roue.

She wadna bake, nor she wadna brew,
For the spoiling o' her comely hue.

She wadna card, nor she wadna spin,
For the shaming o' her gentle kin.

She wadna wash, nor she wadna wring,
For the spoiling o' her golden ring.

The cooper's awa to his wool-pack,
And has laid a sheep-skin on his wife's back.

'It's I'll no' thrash ye, for your proud kin,
But I will thrash my ain sheep-skin.'

'Oh, I will bake, and I will brew,
And never mair think on my comely hue.

'Oh, I will card, and I will spin,
And never mair think on my gentle kin.

'Oh, I will wash, and I will wring,
And never think mair on my golden ring.'

A' ye wha hae gotten a gentle wife
Send ye for the wee cooper o' Fife.

Not known

Queen Mab

This is Mab, the mistress Fairy,
That doth nightly rob the dairy,
And can help or hurt the churning,
As she please without discerning.

She that pinches country wenches,
If they rub not clean their benches,
And with sharper nails remembers
When they rake not up their embers:
But if so they chance to feast her,
In a shoe she drops a tester.

This is she that empties cradles,
Takes out children, puts in ladles:
Trains forth old wives in their slumber,
With a sieve the holes to number;
And then leads them from her burrows,
Home through ponds and water-furrows.

She can start our franklin's[1] daughters,
In their sleep, with shrieks and laughters;
And on sweet St. Anna's night,
Feed them with a promised sight,
Some of husbands, some of lovers,
Which an empty dream discovers.

Ben Jonson

[1] country squire of moderate estate

from The Faerie Queene

Therewith the Giant buckled him to fight,
    Inflamed with scornful wrath and high disdain,
And lifting up his dreadful club on height,
    All armed with ragged snubbes[1] and knotty grain,
    Him thought at first encounter to have slain.
But wise and wary was that noble Peer;
    And, lightly leaping from so monstrous main,
Did fair avoid the violence him near:
It booted nought to think such thunderbolts to bear.

No shame he thought to shun so hideous might:
    The idle stroke enforcing furious way,
Missing the mark of his misaimed sight,
    Did fall to ground, and with his heavy sway
    So deeply dinted in the driven clay,
That three yards deep a furrow up did throw.
    The sad earth, wounded with so sore essay,
Did groan full grievous underneath the blow,
And trembling with strange fear did like an earthquake show.

As when almighty Jove, in wrathful mood,
    To wreak the guilt of mortal sins is bent,
Hurls forth his thundering dart with deadly food
    Enrolled in flames, and smouldering dreariment,
    Through riven clouds and molten firmament;
The fierce three-forked engine, making way,
    Both lofty towers and highest trees hath rent,
And all that might his angry passage stay,
And, shooting in the earth, casts up a mount of clay.

[1] hard knobs

His boisterous club, so buried in the ground,
    He could not rearen up again so light,
But that the knight him at advantage found;
    And, whiles he strove his cumbered club to quight[1]
    Out of the earth, with blade all burning bright
He smote off his left arm, which like a block
    Did fall to ground, deprived of native might;
Large streams of blood out of the trunkèd stock
Forth gushèd, like fresh water stream from riven rock.

Dismayed with so desperate deadly wound,
    And eke impatient of unwonted pain,
He loudly brayed with beastly yelling sound,
    That all the fields rebellowèd again.
    As great a noise, as when in Cymbrian plain
A herd of bulls, whom kindly rage doth sting,
    Do for the milky mothers' want complain,
And fill the fields with troublous bellowing,
And neighbour woods around with hollow murmuring.

Edmund Spenser

The ballad of Richard Peake

This is the tale of Richard Peake,
    Of Tavistock in Devon,
And the fight he fought in Xeres town –
    God rest his soul in Heaven!

[1] set free

I know each pool of Dart and Exe
    Where trout or grayling hide,
I know the moors from sea to sea
    And where the red-deer bide;
I know a tall ship stem to stern,
    What sail to set or strike,
I know to point a culverin
    And how to thrust a pike.
I know the star-way through the night
    And the bodings in the skies,
But many a man knows more than I
    That is not wondrous wise.
I cannot turn a silken phrase,
    Nor make a sonnet sing;
Yet must I write my chronicle
    For my good Lord the King.
A western man and lowly born,
    And early sent to sea –
So simple as my breeding was,
    Let this my record be.

Ye have heard my Lord of Essex
    How he sailed to Cadiz Bay,
With all King Charles' men of war
    Upon a Saturday.
We were sixteen sail of Holland,
    And a hundred of the line,
And I was pricked a volunteer
    Aboard the *Convertine.*
We had stormed the fort and castle
    From rising of the sun,
And long ere noon they landed
    And silenced every gun.

But I was no shore soldier,
    And so on board must bide
What time my Lord of Essex
    Marched up the country-side.

Now it fell on the Monday morning
    I took my leave ashore,
And walked up through the orange groves
    A mile might be, or more.
'Twas said the countryside was bare,
    The country-folk in flight,
A score of miles round Cadiz town,
    And not a Don in sight –
When suddenly a cavalier
    His long sword at the thrust
Came spurring down the narrow way
    With a clatter through the dust.

His steed was checked, his grip was loosed,
    With a flap from my blue cloak;
I clutched the rider by the heel,
    And caught the muffled stroke;
I dragged him down upon his face
    And stripped him where he lay,
I took five silver pieces
    And a horse in that affray.
But while he begged his life in words
    That lisp on English ears,
There stole down through the orange groves
    His squad of musketeers:
And when my hands were bound behind,
    That knight, to his disgrace,
Took back the sword I stripped him of
    And slashed me in the face.

With seven guards on either hand
    And this brave knight before,
They brought me bound and bloody
    In through the city door;
They gored my back with halberds
    And spat into my face;
The urchins called me heathen swine,
    God give them little grace!
They threw me into prison
    So bloodless and so weak,
It needed all their leeches
    To find me strength to speak;
And vain it was my Captain sent
    To ransom Richard Peake.

I saw our frigates hoisting sail
    Upon the seventh day,
And through my dungeon window
    I watched them fade away.
Two Irish monks came every noon
    And wasted pious breath,
Adjuring me from heresy
    Since I must die the death.
And when a week had passed they said
    It was the Governor's mind
That I should thence to Xeres town
    To the torture, they divined.

In Xeres Duke Medina lay
    With many a Count and Earl,
And gravely these good lords were met
    To try the English churl.

It was a pleasant sight to see
    Where they sat in double rows,
Such ruffles and such velvet cloaks
    And slashen sleeves and hose!
The Duke sat at the table's head
    With the King's golden chain –
I mind no finer gentlemen
    Than gentlemen in Spain.
And there and then Medina's self
    Rebuked that craven knight
Who struck the prisoner in the face
    He dared not face in fight.
They plied me well with questions –
    What guns were in the fleet?
What ship was mine? What captain?
    And I answered as was meet.
They asked how strong the fort was
    That watches Plymouth Sound,
And boastfully I lied my best
    As a Devon man was bound.
Quoth one, 'Why spared ye Cadiz?
    Your fleet put back to sea!'
'Who loots,' said I, 'in palaces
    May let the almshouse be.'
But all this while the soldiers round
    Made mirth each time I spoke,
And ugly words for English ears
    Went round the common folk:
Until some jest rang o'er the rest,
    And all those nobles smiled;
Now God forbid that I should stand
    And hear my land reviled.

I said, 'Your king keeps gallant troops
To wear such bands and cuffs,
And they should hold in battle firm
When the starch is in their ruffs.
Yet were I free to pick my choice
From a score of oaken sticks,
I'd stand and play my quarterstaff
For life or death with six.'
'Now, by the rood,' Medina said,
'A braggart though thou be,
I will not take thee at thy word,
But fight thou shalt with three!'

And if I made so bold a face
Be sure it was not pride,
But Richard Peake of Tavistock
Had heard his land belied.
I deemed my death was long resolved,
So basely would not die,
And three to one were heavy odds
For a better man than I.
A halberd was my quarterstaff –
They knocked the blade away,
The iron spike which shod the butt
Stood me in stead that day.
I swung the halberd round my head
And felt my might again,
And I took my stand for England
Against the arch-foe Spain.

Then out stepped three hidalgos,
Steel armoured cap-a-pie,
And lightly sprang into the lists
With a mocking bow to me.
God save my Lord – though I must speak –
It was a pretty fight,

Three long swords thrust and feinted
    In front, to left, to right;
While round their heads the halberd swung
    And as they closed up near,
I snapped two blades - then shortened grip
    And used it as a spear;

I drove it at the third one's breast,
    And a horrid wound it made,
The iron butt went through his heart
    And out by the shoulder-blade.
And now befell a wondrous thing -
    I needs must say again
Earth holds no finer gentlemen
    Than the gentlemen of Spain.

Those nobles rose and clapped their hands:
    The Duke was first to speak,
He bade no man on pain of death
    Lay hands on Richard Peake.
They gave me gold, a band and cuffs,
    This cloak I wear, the ring,
And sent me forth, escorted well
    To see the Spanish King:
And in Madrid on Christmas Day
    I knelt before his sight,
Resolving all his questionings
    With what poor wit I might.
He would have had me bide in Spain
    To serve on shore or sea,
But I've a wife by Tavy side
    And she's got none but me.
Wherefore he pitied my estate
    And pardon free bestowed,
With a hundred pistoles in my scrip
    For charges on the road.

And so I bade Madrid farewell,
    And came without annoy
Through France to Bordeaux haven,
    And thence took ship to Foy.

Now while the Tamar winds to sea,
    And while the Tavy runs,
God bless my old west country,
    And God bless all her sons!
It's not in vain we've tracked the deer
    By dale and moor and fen,
And drunk the morning with our lips,
    And grown up brawny men.
It's not in vain we swam the Sound,
    And tugged the heavy oar,
And braced the nerve and trained the limbs
    That English mothers bore.
And therefore when the fight goes hard,
    And the many meet the few,
She'll still find hands to do the work
    That English lads must do.
So here I render thanks to God,
    Who brought me through the sea,
Across the desert, back again,
    My mother-land, to thee.

This was the tale of Richard Peake
    Of Tavistock in Devon,
And the fight he fought in Xeres town –
    God rest his soul in Heaven!

Lord Rennell of Rodd

Prayer before birth

I am not yet born; O hear me.
Let not the bloodsucking bat or the rat or the stoat or the
    club-footed ghoul come near me.

I am not yet born, console me.
I fear that the human race may with tall walls wall me,
    with strong drugs dope me, with wise lies lure me,
        on black racks rack me, in blood-baths roll me.

I am not yet born; provide me
With water to dandle me, grass to grow for me, trees to
    talk
    to me, sky to sing to me, birds and a white light
        in the back of my mind to guide me.

I am not yet born; forgive me
For the sins that in me the world shall commit, my words
    when they speak me, my thoughts when they think me,
        my treason engendered by traitors beyond me,
            my life when they murder by means of my
                hands, my death when they live me.

I am not yet born; rehearse me
In the parts I must play and the cues I must take when
    old men lecture me, bureaucrats hector me, mountains
        frown at me, lovers laugh at me, the white
            waves call me to folly and the desert calls
                me to doom and the beggar refuses
                    my gift and my children curse me.

I am not yet born; O hear me,
Let not the man who is beast or who thinks he is God
    come near me.

I am not yet born; O fill me
With strength against those who would freeze my
        humanity, would dragoon me into a lethal automaton,
            would make me a cog in a machine, a thing with
                one face, a thing, and against all those
                    who would dissipate my entirety, would
                        blow me like thistledown hither and
                            thither or hither and thither
                                like water held in the
                                    hands would spill me.

Let them not make me a stone and let them not spill me.
Otherwise kill me.

Louis MacNeice

Four orders

I am a trembling leaf
I am a withered arm
I am a sunken reef
I am a trampled worm.

Leaf, be the caterpillar's joy
Arm, enfold the new-born boy
Reef, flower into a coral isle
Worm, fertilise the soil.

Ronald Bottrall

Pilgrim's song

Who would true Valour see,
Let him come hither;
One here will Constant be,
Come Wind, come Weather;
There's no Discouragement
Shall make him once Relent
His first avowed Intent
TO BE A PILGRIM.

Who so beset him round
With dismal Stories,
Do but themselves Confound,
His Strength the more is.
No Lion can him fright;
He'll with a Giant Fight,
But he will have a Right
TO BE A PILGRIM.

Hobgoblin, nor foul Fiend
Can daunt his Spirit;
He knows, he at the end
Shall Life Inherit.
Then fancies fly away,
He'll fear not what men say,
He'll labour Night and Day
TO BE A PILGRIM.

John Bunyan

For his mercy endureth for ever

O give thanks unto the Lord; for he is good:
For his mercy endureth for ever.
O give thanks unto the God of gods:
For his mercy endureth for ever.
O give thanks to the Lord of lords:
For his mercy endureth for ever.
To him who alone doeth great wonders:
For his mercy endureth for ever.
To him that by wisdom made the heavens:
For his mercy endureth for ever.
To him that stretched out the earth above the waters:
For his mercy endureth for ever.
To him that made great lights:
For his mercy endureth for ever.
The sun to rule by day:
For his mercy endureth for ever.
The moon and stars to rule by night:
For his mercy endureth for ever.
O give thanks unto the God of heaven
For his mercy endureth for ever.

from Psalm 136, *Authorised Version of the Bible*

The King of glory shall come in

The earth is the Lord's, and the fulness thereof;
The world, and they that dwell therein.
For he hath founded it upon the seas,
And established it upon the floods.
Who shall ascend into the hill of the Lord?
And who shall stand in his holy place?
He that hath clean hands, and a pure heart;
Who hath not lifted up his soul unto vanity,
Nor sworn deceitfully.
He shall receive the blessing from the Lord,
And righteousness from the God of his salvation.
This is the generation of them that seek him,
That seek thy face, O Jacob.

Lift up your heads, O ye gates;
And be ye lift up, ye everlasting doors;
And the King of glory shall come in.
Who is this King of glory?
The Lord strong and mighty,
The Lord mighty in battle.
Lift up your heads, O ye gates;
Even lift them up, ye everlasting doors;
And the King of glory shall come in.
Who is this King of glory?
The Lord of hosts, he is the King of glory.

Psalm 24,
Authorised Version of the Bible

Magnificat

My soul doth magnify the Lord;
And my spirit hath rejoiced in God my Saviour.
For he hath regarded the lowliness of his handmaiden.
For behold from henceforth
All generations shall call me blessed.
For he that is mighty hath magnified me;
And holy is his Name.
And his mercy is on them that fear him
Throughout all generations.
He hath shewed strength with his arm:
He hath scattered the proud in the imagination of their hearts.
He hath put down the mighty from their seat:
And hath exalted the humble and meek.
He hath filled the hungry with good things:
And the rich he hath sent empty away.
He remembering his mercy hath holpen his servant Israel
As he promised to our forefathers,
Abraham and his seed, for ever.
Glory be to the Father, and to the Son
And to the Holy Ghost,
As it was in the beginning, is now, and ever shall be,
World without end. Amen.

Book of Common Prayer

A living

A man should never earn his living,
if he earns his life he'll be lovely.

A bird
picks up its seeds or little snails
between heedless earth and heaven
in heedlessness.

But, the plucky little sport, it gives to life
song, and chirruping, gay feathers, fluff-shadowed warmth
and all the unspeakable charm of birds hopping and fluttering
 and being birds.
– And we, we get it all from them for nothing.

D H Lawrence

My busconductor

My busconductor tells me
he only has one kidney
and that may soon go on strike
through overwork.
Each busticket
takes on now a different shape
and texture.
He holds a ninepenny single
as if it were a rose
and puts the shilling in his bag
as a child into a gasmeter.

His thin lips
have no quips
for fat factorygirls
and he ignores
the drunk who snores
and the oldman who talks to himself
and gets off at the wrong stop.
He goes gently to the bedroom
of the bus
to collect
and watch familiar shops and pubs passby
(perhaps for the last time?)
The sameold streets look different now
more distinct
as through new glasses.
And the sky
was it ever so blue?

And all the time
deepdown in the deserted busshelter of his mind
he thinks about his journey nearly done.
One day he'll clock on and never clock off
or clock off and never clock on.

Roger McGough

Days

What are days for?
Days are where we live.
They come, they wake us
Time and time over.
They are to be happy in:
Where can we live but days?

Ah, solving that question
Brings the priest and the doctor
In their long coats
Running over the fields.

Philip Larkin

The song of the mad prince

Who said, 'Peacock Pie'?
    The old King to the sparrow:
Who said, 'Crops are ripe'?
    Rust to the barrow:

Who said, 'Where sleeps she now?
    Where rests she now her head,
Bathed in eve's loveliness'?-
    That's what I said.

Who said, 'Ay, mum's the word';
    Sexton to willow:
Who said, 'Green dusk for dreams,
    Moss for a pillow'?
Who said, 'All Time's delight
    Hath she for narrow bed;
Life's troubled bubble broken'?-
    That's what I said.

Walter de la Mare

Death

There is no needle without piercing point.
There is no razor without trenchant blade.
Death comes to us in many forms.

With our feet we walk the goat's earth.
Without our hands we touch God's sky.
Some future day in the heat of noon,
I shall be carried shoulder high
through the village of the dead.
When I die, don't bury me under forest trees,
I fear their thorns.
When I die, don't bury me under forest trees.
I fear the dripping water.
Bury me under the great shade trees in the market,
I want to hear the drums beating
I want to feel the dancers' feet.

Traditional African poem from the Kuba district

Index of first lines

A man should never earn his living 117
At fifteen I went with the army 75
By the North Gate, the wind blows full of sand 68
Came up that cold sea at Cromer like a running grave 17
Call out, Call loud: 'I'm ready! Come and find me! 13
Darkness begins to reign; the louder wind 63
Experienc'd men, inur'd to city ways 30
Forth goes the woodman, leaving unconcerned 23
Give to me the life I love 24
'Good afternoon, Sir Smasham Uppe! 97
Haste thee, Harold, haste thee North! 70
He seemed so certain 'all was going well' 36
Her mother bore her, father cared 14
I am a trembling leaf 112
I am not yet born; O hear me 111
I am the city of two divided cities 32
I found this jaw-bone at the sea's edge 64
I love it well oercanopied in leaves 19
'I really take it very kind 98
In Pilsen 66
In the hot noons I heard the fusillade 3
I sat all morning in the college sick bay 4
In 'thirty-nine, in Poland 79
It is an ancient Mariner 42
It was impossible to leave the town 32
John Gilpin was a citizen 88
Lying in bed in the dark, I hear the bray 18
May I for my own self song's truth reckon 37
Mr Smith, Mr Smith 34
My brother was a pilot 65
My busconductor tells me 117
My father's friend came once to tea 2
My life could have ended then, crouched over the pool 2

My parents kept me from children who were rough 4
My soul doth magnify the Lord 116
Now in contiguous Drops the Flood comes down 31
Now it is almost night; from the bronzey soft sky 27
O Captain! my Captain! our fearful trip is done! 78
O give thanks unto the Lord; for he is good 114
One day on our village in the month of July 76
Outside the house an ash-tree hung its terrible whips 14
Seen from above 16
She had been ill for years and years 8
She kept an antique shop – or it kept her 11
She was sitting on the rough embankment 69
Somebody's knockin' at th' door 9
Stack the cups and clear away 12
The earth is the Lord's and the fulness thereof 115
The king sits in Dunfermline town 38
The snail pushes through a green 18
The splendour falls on castle walls 65
The summer season at Tyne Dock 1
The ten hours' light is abating 28
The white man has brought his war to the beach 67
The winter evening settles down 29
There is no needle without piercing point 120
There was a weasel lived in the sun 25
There was a wee cooper who lived in Fife 99
Therewith the Giant buckled him to fight 102
They that go down to the sea in ships 41
This house has been far out at sea all night 26
This is Mab, the mistress Fairy 101
This is the tale of Richard Peake 103
This winter's weather it waxeth cold 86
What are days for? 118
When I was born on Amman hill 6
Wo said, 'Peacock Pie'? 119
Who would true Valour see 113
'Your father's gone,' my bald headmaster said 5

You know, we French stormed Ratisbon 74
You, without gleam or glint or fire 34